Style and Epoch
Problems of Modern Architecture

OPPOSITIONS BOOKS

Introduction and translation by
Anatole Senkevitch, Jr.
Foreword by Kenneth Frampton

Moisei Ginzburg

Style and Epoch

Published for the Graham Foundation for Advanced Studies
in the Fine Arts, Chicago, Illinois, and
The Institute for Architecture and Urban Studies,
New York, New York, by

The MIT Press
Cambridge, Massachusetts, and London, England

1982

*Library of Congress Cataloging in
Publication Data*
Ginzburg, Moisei Iakovlevich, 1892–1946.
Style and epoch.
(Oppositions Books)
Translation of: Stil' i epokha.
Includes bibliographic references.
1. Architecture and history.
2. Architecture—Philosophy
3. Architecture—Composition,
proportion, etc.
I. Title.
II. Series.
NA2543.H55G5313 1982 720'.1 82-10054
ISBN 0-262-07088-X

Typography by The Old Typosopher in
Century Expanded. Printed and bound by
Halliday Lithograph Corporation in the
United States of America.

*Jacket illustration: Caprone triplane.
From the title page of the original
Russian edition.*

Other titles in the OPPOSITIONS
BOOKS series:

**Essays in Architectural Criticism:
Modern Architecture and
Historical Change**
Alan Colquhoun
Preface by Kenneth Frampton

Spoken into the Void
Adolf Loos
Introduction by Aldo Rossi
Translation by Jane O. Newman
and John H. Smith

The Architecture of the City
Aldo Rossi
Introduction by Peter Eisenman
Translation by Diane Ghirardo
and Joan Ockman

A Scientific Autobiography
Aldo Rossi
Postscript by Vincent Scully
Translation by Lawrence Venuti

NA
2543
.H55
G5313
1982

OPPOSITIONS BOOKS

Editors
Peter Eisenman
Kenneth Frampton

Executive Editor
Joan Ockman

Assistant Editor
Thomas Mellins

Design
Massimo Vignelli

Design Coordinator
Abigail Sturges

Production
Heidi King

Contents

Jacket of the original edition of Style and
Epoch, *designed by Alexander A. Vesnin.
From A. G. Chiniakov,* Brat'ia Vesniny
(Moscow, 1970), p. 71.

One of the more surprising things about this seminal treatise published in 1924 is that it has taken nearly sixty years to issue an English version of a text which evidently played a major role in the development of Soviet architecture. This lapsus is all the more incomprehensible given that Ginzburg's place in the Modern Movement stems as much from his leadership and theoretical writing as it does from his equally extensive activity as an architect. Indeed, Ginzburg belongs to that rare class of accomplished designers who, without relinquishing their vocation, find time for polemics and for the formulation of a coherent body of theory. Should one look for his equivalent today, one would only find such a figure in Italy, Germany, or Japan, and it is possible that the very range of Ginzburg's achievement—the extent of his erudition, the lucidity of his theory, and the fertility of his practice—goes a long way toward accounting for the belatedness of this translation, since such a combination of theory and practice has never been accorded great respect in Anglo-Saxon circles.

This prejudice may be also be detected in the current reading of his career, where the tendency has been to recognize him mostly for his founding of the OSA group and his editorship of its magazine *Sovremennaia Arkhitektura*, without giving sufficient credit to his practice and to the pioneering housing studies made for the Building Committee of the USSR under his auspices. The fact is that he entered some fourteen competitions between 1923 and 1927, and in so doing produced a series of remarkable projects, of which two, both designed with I. F. Milinis, became canonical Constructivist works: the Narkomfin experimental housing block, brought to completion in Novinsky Boulevard, Moscow, in 1930, and the Alma-Ata government building, completed the following year, the latter being one of the earliest Russian buildings to reflect the full influence of Le Corbusier's syntax and method. The Narkomfin block, on the other hand, despite Corbusian overtones, asserts the independence of Ginzburg's thought, his determination to evolve a collective housing form appropriate to Soviet conditions, rather than mimic the progressive but nonetheless bourgeois housing types developed by Le Corbusier.

The Narkomfin block was a culmination of four years of intensive development, beginning with Ginzburg's more conventional Malaia Bronnaia block, completed in Moscow in 1927, and continuing with the research work carried out by a team of architects working under his direction. Between 1928 and 1930 Ginzburg, together with M. Barshch, V. Vladimirov, A. Pasternak, and Sum-Sik, designed and tested a number of alternative prototypes in order to arrive at an appropriate and economical typology for the standard form of Soviet residential development, the so-called *dom-kommuna*, whose optimum socio-architectural form preoccupied the Soviet avant-garde throughout the twenties. The generic, split-level Stroikom section, which emerged as the most prototypical consequence of this research, clearly antedates Le Corbusier's famous cross-over duplex unit, first projected in 1934 and finally realized in the Marseille Unité d'habitation of 1952. Yet despite the radical form of the Narkomfin block (its assembly of Type F and Type K Stroikom units into a six-story slab linked by an interior street to a communal canteen, gymnasium, library, nursery, and roof garden), Ginzburg remained aware that such a commune could only be humanly successful if it was induced rather than imposed.

Ginzburg was as much temperamentally as ideologically inclined to the ideal of the collective, for as S. O. Khan-Magomedov has remarked, he was at his best as a designer when working collaboratively, and the more interesting projects of his career were invariably arrived at jointly, from his avant-gardist Green City proposal for the de-urbanization of the existing population of Moscow, designed in 1930 with Barshch, to his somewhat conservative proposal for the Palace of the Soviets, designed in 1932 with the German architect Gustav Hassenpflug. This project, together with Ginzburg's entry for the Sverdlovsk Theater competition of the previous year, served to inaugurate his Neo-Suprematist style, a manner which was patently influenced by the work of the young OSA protégé Ivan Leonidov.

As Anatole Senkevitch indicates, Ginzburg's *Style and Epoch* unavoidably invites comparison with Le Corbusier's *Vers une architecture* of 1923, by which it was surely influenced, since Ginzburg would have read this book when it first appeared in installments in the pages of *L'Esprit Nouveau*. However, as in all such comparisons, the differences are of greater consequence than the similarities, and these are perhaps most dramatically indicated by the respective choice of illustrations. While both texts are illuminated with futurist engineering images, that is to say, with the grain silos, factories, ships, and aircraft of the turn of the century, they ultimately use this material to different ends. Where Ginzburg features battleships, welded-steel railway termini, and wood-framed industrial cooling towers, Le Corbusier excludes the warship in favor of the bourgeois transatlantic liner. Similarly, while both men find the North American grain elevator and the Fiat works at Turin to be exemplary of the new epoch and its style, they differ over the issue of wood construction, Le Corbusier restricting the new architecture to steel and concrete and Ginzburg admitting into the canon not only anonymous industrial timber structures but more specifically the work of his more "primitive" Constructive colleagues, such as, for instance, Konstantin Melnikov, whose Makhorka pavilion for the All-Russian Agricultural Exhibition held in Moscow in 1923 is prominently featured, as is V. A. Shchuko's cafe for the same exhibition.

Ginzburg's feeling for construction also has its phantasmagoric, Piranesian overtones, as we may judge from his inclusion of drawings by E. I. Norvert for a modern power station, presumably meant to demonstrate an ideal syntax in which concrete and steel would be equally mixed. Of course, both men accord equal importance to the airplane as the bearer of the new spirit, even if they choose to illustrate different models. However, where Le Corbusier cites the bourgeois automobile along with the liner and the biplane as the ultimate demiurges of modernity in *Eyes Which Do Not See*, Ginzburg illustrates his thesis of modern dynamism by advancing the locomotive as the exemplary functional form.

Like *Towards a New Architecture*, *Style and Epoch* accepts and wholeheartedly welcomes the universal civilizing force of modern technology, a force which in czarist Russia was already making the continuation of local culture increasingly difficult. Ginzburg's adherence to the "law of continuity" and his essentially Darwinian, not to say "genetic," concept of the evolution of style was altogether more naturalistic as a model of change than Le Corbusier's dualistic concept of the way in which modern architectural culture would be brought into being. I am referring to Le Corbusier's dialectical idea of the "Engineer's Aesthetic and Architecture," about which his major theoretical work is structured. Where Ginzburg embraces the notion of an all-determining machinist *Zeitgeist*, Le Corbusier, while championing the scientific industrial world, still posits the necessary presence of a poetic "will-to-form," which would on occasion be capable of raising the calculated elegance of engineering form to a higher, Neoplatonic plane.

8

This idealistic model of the generation of form was inconceivable to Ginzburg, since he could no longer think of the architect as a figure who was professionally independent from the engineer. As far as he was concerned (and he had himself been trained both as an engineer and an architect), architectural practice had by the twenties already become absorbed by engineering, and the primary task now was for the architectural theorist (namely himself) to formulate a new theory of form to account for this absorption. He had in fact prepared the ground for this acceptance in his earlier *Rhythm in Architecture* of 1923, in which he directly posited a theory of architecture based on the notion of evolving formal rhythms, a theory in some ways comparable to such formal systems as those advanced by N. A. Ladovsky in the VKHUTEMAS and the method which later would be articulated by Iakov Chernikhov in his books *Architecture and Machines* and *Architectural Fantasies*, published in 1931 and 1933 respectively.

As the spectrum of his publications would indicate, from *Rhythm in Architecture* of 1923 to *Housing* of 1934, Ginzburg's development ran the full historical gamut, from the young practitioner and theorist reacting to his training as a classical stylist in Italy to someone polemically involved with the economic optimization of the living cell, the pursuit of the Soviet equivalent of the *Existenzminimum*. Ginzburg the technocrat and superfunctionalist reaches this apotheosis in the second chapter of *Housing*; here, packing his argument with formulas and calculations of the most abstruse kind, he treats with whatever ergonomic optimum was deemed appropriate for a certain range of households at a fixed cost. Despite the inexplicably wasteful one-and-a-half story height of the Stroikom units, this program resembles the Taylorist ideal of A. K. Gastev's Moscow-based Central Labor Institute. *Style and Epoch*, on the other hand, attempts to demonstrate the course repeated throughout history of the birth, maturation, degeneration, and death of any given style, thereby affording its author the opportunity to argue at the conclusion of his thesis that the Soviet Union was standing at the threshold of an emerging new expression, only this time one that would be formulated at a universal level. Ginzburg's own first forays into evolving this style were tentative and eclectic in the extreme, as we may judge from the heavy pastiche of Byzantine and Neoclassical forms which characterizes his entry for the Palace of Labor competition of 1923. However, by the time of the Orgametals Building competition of 1926, he had become a fully converted functionalist. Finally, by 1933 with his work on Kislovodsk Sanitorium in the Crimea, he would embrace a highly rationalized form of Social Realist architecture, which was then to characterize his ensuing career as a practicing architect up to his death in 1946.

Thus, while *Style and Epoch* formulates the ideology of a style that endured little more than six years, it nonetheless remains a compelling and significant testimony to the promise of a modern architecture whose liberative potential remains as valid today as when it was first proclaimed.

Kenneth Frampton

**Introduction:
Moisei Ginzburg and the
Emergence of a Constructivist
Theory of Architecture**

Stil' i epokha [Style and Epoch], published in 1924 by Moisei Iakovlevich Ginzburg, is the first and most important elucidation of early Constructivist theory in Soviet architecture. It presents seminal concepts which were later elaborated into a fully developed doctrine of Constructivist architecture, but which at the time of the book's writing were only beginning to be crystallized. In this sense, Ginzburg's treatise reveals a theory in process of formulation. Yet at the same time, through its author's lucid observations on an impressive sweep of historical, theoretical, and formal problems, it also brings to light the vibrant intellectual content of Constructivist architectural thought. Few writings associated with the movement demonstrate so well the full depth and breadth of Constructivist theory, or the extent to which its aims and ideals were central to those of the Modern Movement.

It may facilitate a fuller understanding of this compelling but not always easy treatise to set it into its proper historical and theoretical perspective. In one sense, of course, it needs neither explanation nor commentary: it was published without the help of either, the time and circumstances of its publication providing both. Moreover, a number of the aspirations addressed by the book are strikingly in accord with those of Ginzburg's modernist contemporaries in Western Europe. Indeed, its conception of a scientifically determined and historically predestined architecture, one that is socially useful and embodies the innate spirit of the time, makes *Style and Epoch* one of the theoretical touchstones of the Modern Movement.

Style and Epoch, Ginzburg's second book on architecture and his theoretical *chef d'oeuvre*, propelled him to sudden prominence in the Soviet Union. Its penetrating analysis of stylistic change in architecture was hailed by art historians as a model of scholarly art criticism.[1] At the same time, its comprehensive effort to conceptualize aspects of the "new architecture" for the young socialist state prompted many Soviet architects to clarify their own positions on the subject. The book's paramount importance, however, stems from its instrumental role in coalescing the basic strains of the subsequent Constructivist doctrine in Soviet architecture.

Although Ginzburg's treatise conveys his tacit approval of the essential thrust of Constructivism, it refrains from avowing any direct connection to the Constructivist movement in Soviet art, which had come into being in 1921; none of the early Constructivist pronouncements had made any significant references to architecture, save for the rudimentary position adopted in Aleksei Gan's essay *Konstruktivizm* of 1922. In *Style and Epoch* Ginzburg largely goes his own way in formulating a positivist program for a "constructive" architecture, adapting salient aspects of the post-1921 Constructivist ideology of a utilitarian industrial, or "productive," art to his own conception of the creative process in architecture. Ginzburg's ideas, with their immediate antecedents in both Western theory and Soviet criticism, proved seminal to the development of the Constructivist architectural movement, of which Ginzburg emerged as the co-founder and chief theoretician with the founding in 1925 of the Society of Modern Architects (OSA).[2]

Ginzburg's book is a remarkable synthesis of a utopian conception of the mechanized world, a materialist concern for the social and technical meaning of architecture, and a scholarly grasp of contemporary architectural and aesthetic theory. Its lofty and grandiose approach to architectural problems appears in striking contrast to the more pragmatic tone of later Constructivist writing, much of it produced by Ginzburg himself at a time when his group was seeking to improve the technical standards of Soviet building. The earlier approach, however, was a product of the moment in which the book was written and of Ginzburg's corresponding cast of mind, one still detached from the immediate concerns of architectural practice.

The years immediately following the Russian Revolution had produced an active avant-garde movement and an intense burst of theoretical and creative activity in every realm of art. Numerous artists and critics praised the new revolutionary developments in rhapsodic terms and sought to systematize their aesthetic ideals into cogent programs for the creation of a truly "new" art, one fully capable of materializing in appropriate artistic form the projected socio-economic ideals of the revolutionary epoch. *Style and Epoch* epitomizes the programmatic writing that proliferated in Soviet avant-garde and culture in the early post-revolutionary years. At the same time, it formulates more comprehensively than the writings of any of Ginzburg's Soviet contemporaries a deeply held modernist commitment, something which many felt but none expressed as eloquently.

In Soviet architecture, the absence of any significant opportunity to build during the post-revolutionary period of economic dislocation made the early twenties a time well suited for reflection and determination of purpose. Given the uncertainty of the times, Ginzburg's book may be seen as a momentary withdrawal from a reality in process of transformation in order to postulate new theoretical premises for the fundamental regeneration of architecture. It represents a decisive attempt to define the key role of architecture in the new socialist society, one which would marshal the socially and technically rationalized processes of architecture for the vital task of organizing and giving form to the new way of life.

The fact that *Style and Epoch* is the first statement of Constructivist theory in Soviet architecture accounts in part for the book's somewhat transitional character. At the same time, its vacillation between historical detachment and theoretical involvement indicates that the writing of this treatise marks a transition in Ginzburg's own career. Ginzburg attempted to reconcile his obvious flair for and attachment to architectural history with his newly aroused sensibilities as a practitioner who wished to extrapolate and apply history's programmatic implications to the creation of contemporary architecture.

Ginzburg's penchant for historical analysis and determination to set forth a comprehensive theoretical rationale for design principles were products of a keen intellect and erudition, buttressed by an abundant self-assurance. At the same time, the impressive sweep of his professionalism was sustained by a broad cultural and literary background and a breadth and sophistication that distinguished all the leading members of the cultural intelligentsia. In Russia this intellectual class was intrinsically involved with Westernization and the assimilation of Western cultural values and rationalist thought. Adopting a secular and broadly liberal outlook, it absorbed French and especially German positivist thought, a monist view of nature and societal processes, and a utilitarian conception of aesthetics in relation to the material world.[3] Although such materialism was displaced at the turn of the century by a philosophical idealism coming from the various neo-Kantian schools that had penetrated Russia by the 1890s, materialism, as initially defined in *Style and Epoch*, nonetheless remained the essential determinant of Ginzburg's architectural philosophy. That philosophy evolved in response to a wide range of influences and stimuli that Ginzburg ex-

1. This assessment was made by A. A. Sidorov, President of the Art Criticism Section of the Institute of Archaeology and Art Criticism in Moscow, in his "Iskusstvoznanie za 10 let v SSSR" [Art Criticism in the USSR During the Past Ten Years], *Trudy sektsii iskusstvoznaniia*, vol. 2 (Moscow, 1928), p. 12. In an earlier review of *Style and Epoch* art historian Vladimir V. Zgura, though disagreeing with some of Ginzburg's assertions, hailed his book as a major contribution to stylistic theory in Soviet art scholarship; see Zgura, *Pechat' i revoliutsiia*, no. 2 (March–April 1925), pp. 287-89.
2. Between 1926 and 1930 the OSA published the journal *S.A. (Sovremennaia arkhitektura)* [S.A. (Modern Architecture)], of which Ginzburg and Alexander Vesnin were editors-in-chief; that the OSA was the only movement with its own sustained publication accounts in no small measure for its gradual ascendancy in Soviet architecture during this period. As the movement's chief theoretician, Ginzburg published a series of articles in *S.A.* amplifying earlier concepts and postulating new ones. Conceived in terms of their specific application to architectural practice, these articles focus on the promulgation of what Ginzburg and the Constructivists termed the "functional method" of design. Together with *Style and Epoch* they encompass the essential elements of the full-fledged Constructivist doctrine in Soviet architecture. These writings will be included in a compendium of translated documents pertaining to modern Soviet architecture being prepared for publication by the present author. They are discussed in my "Trends in Soviet Architectural Thought, 1917–1932: The Growth and Decline of the Constructivist and Rationalist Movements" (Ph.D. dissertation, Cornell University, 1974), chap. 4.
3. A good overview is Richard Pipes, "The Historical Evolution of the Russian Intelligentsia," in *The Russian Intelligentsia*, ed. Richard Pipes (New York: Columbia Univ. Press, 1961), pp. 47-62. Other essays in this volume focus on various aspects of the Russian intelligentsia both before and after the Revolution.

11

perienced in the course of his varied education and early professional life.

Ginzburg's Education and Early Career

Moisei Iakovlevich Ginzburg (1892–1946) was born in Minsk, the capital of Belorussia (now Belorussian S.S.R.), into an architect's family. Little is known of his youth, save that it was spent in the relatively provincial atmosphere of his home town. Here Ginzburg was subjected to numerous influences that proved important in laying the foundations of his later development. His avid reading of books on art history cultivated a lasting interest in the subject; lessons taken from a local artist likewise instilled in him a love of drawing and painting. It was his architect father, however, who most stimulated Ginzburg's early interest in architecture, allowing his son to become increasingly involved in his architectural practice during young Moisei's school years. Following completion of his secondary education at Minsk, Ginzburg went abroad for his architectural training. After brief periods at the Ecole des Beaux-Arts in Paris and the academy at Toulouse, which were abandoned for unknown reasons, Ginzburg entered the architectural faculty of the Accademia di Belli Arti in Milan, where he studied under one of the leading teachers there, Professor Moretti. Upon receiving his diploma from the Milan academy in 1914, he returned to Russia, where he proceeded to supplement his classical architectural education with a degree in architectural engineering taken at the Riga Polytechnical Institute, from which he graduated in 1917.[4]

Khan's Mosque in Eupatoria, the Crimea.

Former Dervish monastery in Eupatoria.

Former mosque in the Theodosian region of the Crimea.
From Ginzburg, "Tatarskoe iskusstvo v Krymu," Sredi kollektsionerov, no. 1 (1922).

Ginzburg's years abroad enabled him to travel widely and become acquainted with the latest trends in architecture and aesthetic theory. He began to reject the inhibiting limitations of his classical training at the Milan academy, where "deviations from an almost archaeological reproduction of historical styles were not tolerated."[5] As he subsequently lamented in *Style and Epoch*, the effect of such an approach was to stifle students' enthusiasm for modernity, while at the same time isolating them from the true spirit of the creations of the past. His own enthusiasm for modernity during his Milan years ran to Art Nouveau (he executed a student project in the style much to his studio master's displeasure) and an admiration for the work of Frank Lloyd Wright. Years later he also recalled "what an incredible impression the modern automobile in front of the archbishop's palace in Milan made on me at the time."[6] As this recollection suggests, he had acquired first-hand knowledge of Italian Futurism and of the Nuovo Tendenze faction formed by the young architects Antonio Sant'Elia and Mario Chiattone. Yet even though he was influenced by the Futurist insistence that modern art and architecture had to be inspired by the achievements of science and technology and to reflect the dynamism of modern life, he found Marinetti's and Sant'Elia's wholesale rejection of the cultural heritage of the past to be untenable and symptomatic of creative impotence.[7]

Although Ginzburg never refers in his writing to his experience at the Riga Polytechnical Institute, it is doubtful that he could have ventured so detailed an analysis of the operating dynamics and architectonic implications of the machine and engineering structures in *Style and Epoch* without the benefit of its technical curriculum. His own vision of the architect as one endowed with a "constructive sensibility," a feeling predicated on an understanding of the laws of statics and mechanics, obviously relates more to the engineering emphasis of his polytechnical training than to his classical education at the Milan academy. And yet the beneficial discipline of both modes of professional education are equally apparent in Ginzburg's work, their effective constituents being synthesized in his broadly based approach to problems of architectural history, theory, and practice.

With the completion of his engineering studies in 1917, Ginzburg went south to the Crimea, where he spent the next four years. Isolated from the cultural and revolutionary mainstream of the fledgling Soviet state, the Crimean peninsula witnessed many battles of the civil war that followed the revolution; several Tatar nationalist and Russian Bolshevik and anti-Bolshevik factions existed there from 1917 to 1920. Ginzburg recalled his Crimea period as one of "inner struggle with the traditions and canons of the severely classical school I had assimilated in Italy."[8] His first undertaking there involved the design, with N. A. Kopeliovich, of the Lokshin House in Eupatoria (pl. 28). This house seems to have been Ginzburg's declaration of independence from the academy, with its hint of the Prairie Style of Frank Lloyd Wright and discernible *Sezessionsstil* overtones in the fenestration and the severe modeling of mass. The greater part of his stay in the Crimea, however, was taken up with heading a newly established office for the preservation of artistic and cultural monuments and with investigating Tatar folk architecture in the Crimea, on which he published a series of articles.

The spontaneous eclecticism of the Tatar vernacular supplied yet another opportunity for dissipating the influence of the academy. The Crimea afforded Ginzburg a chance to study those anonymous structures which have always evolved organically as an expedient but expressive response to their immediate environment. These studies were undertaken too late to find reflection in the Lokshin House, although they later helped shape the regional overtones of the Crimean Pavilion which Ginzburg designed for the First Agricultural and Cottage Industries Exhibition in Moscow of 1923. Although he subsequently abandoned his enthusiasm for the vernacular and never promoted it as a source of inspiration for modern architecture, he nonetheless perceived it to be a manifestation of the role of expediency as a positive, organic determinant of form; it was an aspect whose presence he was later to extol in industrial architecture. His description of the spontaneous, impulsive character of Tatar folk architecture, "rushing along a natural course, following its bends and irregularities, adding one motif to another with a picturesque spontaneity that conceals a distinct creative order,"[9] anticipated the vivid language he was later to employ in *Style and Epoch* to convey the dynamism of the industrial plant. The latter's forms, too, were seen to respond naturally to exigencies that had nothing to do with aesthetic considerations as such, but which nevertheless engendered compelling forms.

In 1921 Ginzburg left the Crimea and returned to Moscow, which thereafter became the base of his career. At first his activities were devoted almost entirely to pedagogical and scholarly work. He taught architectural history and theory courses at the Moscow Higher Technical Institute (MVTI) and at the VKHU-TEMAS, or Higher State Artistic-Technical Studios, soon emerging as an influential young pedagogue in Moscow. His commitment to scholarly work was recognized and broadened with his election to the State Academy of Artistic Sciences in 1924. In that year he headed the Academy's expedition to Central Asia to study Uzbek housing and establish a museum of antiquity and folk art. In 1925 he accompanied another Academy expedition, this time to Turkey for the purpose of studying Byzantine and Moslem architecture.

Ginzburg's pedagogical and scholarly activity thus left him little time for design work. His only projects of this period are his 1923 Crimean pavilion, employing

4. The Riga Polytechnical Institute had relocated to Moscow during the war years. For biographical information on Ginzburg, see Selim O. Khan-Magomedov, *M. Ia. Ginzburg* (Moscow: Stroiizdat, 1972), pp. 7-8. Cf. "Pamiati M. Ia. Ginzburga" [To the Memory of M. Ia. Ginzburg], *Arkhitektura SSSR*, no. 12 (1946). p. 53.

5. Moisei Ia. Ginzburg, "Put' sovetskogo arkhitektora" [The Path of a Soviet Architect], *Arkhitektura SSSR*, no. 10 (1937), p. 71.

6. Ibid. This comment recalls a similar remark by Filippo Tommaso Marinetti in his "Foundation Manifesto of Futurism," published in *Le Figaro*, Feb. 20, 1909.

7. Ginzburg's ambivalence toward Italian Futurism is somewhat reminiscent of that manifested earlier by the Russian Futurists, who had emerged in 1910 under the leadership of the poet-artists Vladimir Mayakovsky and David Burliuk. Like their Italian predecessors, the Russian Futurists had adopted industrial and urban elements as the leitmotif of their art, employing them to express the new reality of an industrialized world. By the time of Marinetti's visit to Russia in the winter of 1914, however, the Russian movement had cooled appreciably toward Italian Futurism, believing that its own accomplishments had largely overtaken those of the Italians. See Vladimir Markov, *Russian Futurism: A History* (Berkeley-Los Angeles: Univ. of California Press, 1968), pp. 147-53.

8. Ginzburg, "Tvorcheskie otchety" [Career Profiles], *Arkhitektura SSSR*, no. 3 (1935), p. 8.

9. Ginzburg, "Tatarskoe iskusstvo v Krymu" [Tatar Art in the Crimea], *Sredi kollektsionerov*, nos. 11-12 (1921), p. 36. This article inaugurated a series that Ginzburg published on the subject in this journal. Subsequent articles appeared as follows: no. 1 (1922), pp. 19-25; no. 3 (1922), pp. 18-26; nos. 7-8 (1922), pp. 22-28; and nos. 1-2 (1924), pp. 22-26.

10. Ginzburg, "Tvorcheskie otchety," p. 8.

11. That Alexander Vesnin befriended Ginzburg in 1923 and brought him into the Productivist circle of avant-garde artists is noted by Roman Ia. Khiger, an associate of Ginzburg's in the OSA; see Khiger, "M. Ia. Ginzburg: Put' teoretika i mastera" [M. Ia. Ginzburg: The Path of a Theoretician and Master], *Sovetskaia arkhitektura*, no. 15 (1963), p. 119.

A primitive minaret in Bakhchisarai.

A traditional Crimean house in Eupatoria. From Ginzburg, "Tatarskoe iskusstvo v Krymu," Sredi kollektsionerov, *no. 1 (above) and no. 3 (below), 1922.*

regional motifs, and the project developed in collaboration with A. Z. Grinberg for the 1922–1923 competition for the Palace of Labor in Moscow (pls. 23, 24), an exuberant but undistinguished assembly of monumental forms. Like the Lokshin house, neither project helped to crystallize a Constructivist sensibility; this object was first realized in the competition projects made by the brothers Alexander A., Victor A., and Leonid A. Vesnin for the Palace of Labor and the Leningrad Pravda building in 1923 and 1924 respectively. Yet despite the fact that it was the Vesnins and not Ginzburg who established the initial aspects of a Constructivist architecture, it was Ginzburg's corresponding theoretical texts, culminating in *Style and Epoch*, that imbued this early Constructivist architecture with its fundamental intellectual and theoretical content.

That Ginzburg ventured into such an ambitious undertaking indicates the extent to which academic activity alone could not fulfill the breadth of his professional commitment. The theoretical atmosphere which he encountered upon returning to Moscow in 1921 had become sharply polarized by contending avant-garde factions. In addition to his primary pursuits, he also began "accumulating numerous new elements that helped shape my creative consciousness."[10] Soon he became immersed in the heated debates at the VKHUTEMAS and elsewhere in Moscow concerning the various tendencies and alternatives for a modern architecture.

The friendship developed in 1923 with Alexander Vesnin and his brothers Victor and Leonid proved most auspicious in this regard, as it brought Ginzburg into the orbit of those aesthetic ideas which were beginning to give rise to a Constructivist sensibility in architecture.[11] This friendship created the organizational nucleus of the Constructivist movement in Soviet architecture, which emerged fully fledged in 1925 with the founding of the Society of Modern Architects (OSA), of which Alexander Vesnin was president and Ginzburg and Victor Vesnin were vice-presidents. As a member of the pioneer circle of Constructivist artists and critics that clustered around the journal *LEF* from 1923 onward, after the dissolution of the Institute of Artistic Culture (INKHUK), Alexander Vesnin soon emerged as a major innovator in the field of Constructivist art.

Trained as an architect at the Institute of Civil Engineers in St. Petersburg, Alexander Vesnin was first exposed to avant-garde art in 1912–1914 while working in Vladmir Tatlin's Moscow studio, known as the Towers. After the revolution he became active in the creation of agit-prop street decorations, and in September 1921 he joined with fellow INKHUK Constructivists Alexander Rodchenko, Varvara Stepanova, Alexandra Exter, and Liubov Popova in participating in the *5 x 5 = 25* exhibition, which proclaimed the death of easel painting and heralded the Productivist ideals of the emerging Constructivist movement. It was as a stage designer, however, that Alexander Vesnin emerged as a major force in Constructivist art, a fact which had profound implications for architecture. A succession of stage sets, culminating in a brilliant metaphorical rendering of the modern industrialized city, created for Tairov's staging of G. K. Chesterton's *The Man Who Was Thursday* (1923) at the Moscow Chamber Theater (pl. 17), foreshadowed the specific Vesnin elaboration of the Constructivist sensibility which would manifest itself in architectural projects executed between 1923 and 1925.

For Ginzburg, the years 1922–1923 entailed a concerted assimilation of the latest ideas on modern architecture as elaborated both in the Soviet Union and abroad. He first became aware of the foreign tendencies through a series of European journals, including the Czech magazine *Stavba*, the French publication *L'Esprit Nouveau*, the Polish *Blok*, and the Dutch *De Stijl*, which had started to make their way to the Soviet Union, as well as through the trilingual magazine *Veshch/ Gegenstand/Object*; the latter had been founded in Berlin in 1922 by El Lissitzky and Ilya Ehrenburg for the purpose of presenting the various tendencies of the Soviet avant-garde and demonstrating their connection to similar trends in Western Europe. This was a period in which Ginzburg was increasingly consumed by the task of establishing "those key factors that would help determine the new course" of Soviet architecture.[12]

12. Ginzburg, "Tvorcheskie otchety," p. 8.
13. Ginzburg, *Ritm v arkhitekture* (Moscow: Sredi kollektsionerov, 1923), p. 9.
14. Ibid., p. 71.

Early Writings

The course of the new architecture gradually became clarified for Ginzburg through a series of publications inaugurated by his initial theoretical work *Ritm v arkhitekture* [Rhythm in Architecture] and culminating in *Style and Epoch*. Written in 1922 and published the following year, *Rhythm in Architecture*, a scholarly exposition of his theory of architectural composition, already yields important insights into his theoretical framework. In 1923 his growing reputation in Moscow architectural circles as a progressive and erudite pedagogue secured him the position of editor-in-chief of the short-lived journal *Arhkitektura* [Architecture], which was published by the venerable Moscow Architectural Society. The two editorials which he produced for this journal adumbrated his emerging views on the essential nature of modern architecture. Already polemical in tone, they outlined the main themes which he would subsequently develop in *Style and Epoch*. Finally, two other articles, published concurrently with the writing of *Style and Epoch*, gave a more explicit assessment of the comparative state of modern architecture in the early twenties as manifested in the 1923 Moscow Agricultural Exhibition and in Western Europe.

Rhythm in Architecture is a penetrating examination of the manifestations of rhythm as an aspect of architectural composition from antiquity to modern times, and it is significant for what it reveals about Ginzburg's views concerning architecture's potential for broad cultural significance. Indeed, for Ginzburg, rhythm represented nothing less than the veritable lifeblood of the universe: "We encounter its laws in the movement of the planetary system, in the person who is toiling, in the gesticulations of a wild animal, in the flowing current of a river. No matter what science we turn to, what life we consider, we see manifestations of rhythm everywhere."[13] Rhythm thus was a manifestation of the universal dynamics of movement; animating societal processes ranging from human labor to aesthetic pleasure, it emanated "from the organic essence of mankind."

Ginzburg's treatise on rhythm also clearly reveals his emerging historical consciousness and his views on the dialectical significance of architectural history. Both were to inform his approach to *Style and Epoch*. He believed that architectural history was to be understood and not imitated, and that its lessons were to be derived not so much from the past monuments themselves as from the principles that could be abstracted from them. This belief is reflected in his definition of style, which he regarded as transcending the aspects of visible form. "Architectural style," he wrote, "is an independent world, a distinct and indestructible system of laws explaining and justifying everything within it. To comprehend style is to discern these laws, to fathom each element of form and the compositional methods which help create a living architectural language."[14] Moreover, a history of styles, like any other history, had to be objective; there could be no question of "superior" or "inferior" styles, given that all styles even-

15

15. Ibid., p. 116.
16. Ginzburg, "Estetika sovremennosti" [The Aesthetics of Modernity], *Arkhitektura*, nos. 1-2 (1923), p. 3.
17. Ginzburg, "Staroe i novoe," *Arkhitektura*, nos. 3-5 (1923), p. 3.
18. Ibid.

tually grow obsolete under the impact of creative forces which then necessarily give rise to other styles. Consequently, he concluded, pointing the way to the central argument of *Style and Epoch*, "the problem of modern architecture is to seek out those elements of form and the laws for combining them that will manifest the rhythmic pulse beat of our days."[15]

In his first *Arkhitektura* editorial, entitled "Estetika sovremennosti" [The Aesthetics of Modernity] and marking his debut as a polemicist and avowed proselytizer of modern architecture, Ginzburg confidently proclaimed, "If prior to the war and revolution we could still count on the success of our excursions into vagaries of the Renaissance and classical modes, then surely the past few years have thoroughly convinced us of the simple truth that it is much easier to move forward when one is facing in the same direction."[16] He further asserted that however fragmentary and incomplete the new architectural ideas might be, the very advocacy of a new architecture indicated that a significant and undeniable change had already overtaken the modern aesthetic sensibility. This change, whether for good or ill, was fundamentally conditioned by modern scientific and technological progress, which was epitomized by the perfecting of utilitarian performance through the organizational efficiency of the machine and mechanized methods of production. Anticipating the argument that constitutes the substance of the "manifesto" section of *Style and Epoch*, he maintained that elements of the new style were already discernible, not in traditional building types but in those industrial and engineering structures which had become the most compelling paradigms for a modern architecture.

In his second editorial in *Arkhitektura*, entitled "Staroe i novoe" [The Old and the New], Ginzburg condemned the emerging cliquishness and fragmentation of Soviet art into innumerable "isms," asserting that such a confused state of affairs had arisen out of the dearth of viable artistic ideas capable of "synthesizing the genuine spirit of modernity." This fragmentation was attributable to the antagonism of two basic opposing camps: those who venerated the architectural heritage of the past and could not divorce themselves from its formal influence and those who openly disdained the past in their uncompromising quest for a new architecture. Dismissing both extremes as equally counterproductive, he postulated a middle course which he regarded to be a synthesis of "the genuine spirit of modernity." This synthesis, which underlay the concept of stylistic evolution elaborated in *Style and Epoch*, was predicated on the interactive laws of "continuity" and "independence." Both laws, Ginzburg argued, were involved in the evolution of any new style. The law of continuity enriched the architect's conceptual repository with the architectural experience of the past. The law of independence, on the other hand, encouraged the development of viable new ideas by filtering them through "those forms of life that surround the artist, imbuing creativity with a fresh sharpness and feeling for the rhythm of modernity without which art simply ceases to be art."[17] Ginzburg concluded the editorial with a ringing affirmation of his own unswerving support for modernism and the quest for a "new style": "Being certain that we are entering into a new phase in the development of a *new style*, which has every right to a self-sustaining aesthetic, a different understanding of form, and an independent sense of beauty, we deem it imperative to further in every possible way the revelation of the true face of this new world."[18]

Although Ginzburg promised that subsequent issues already in preparation would be devoted to "problems of modern form," the issue in which this editorial appeared proved to be the journal's last. Those problems were to be addressed and developed in *Style and Epoch* the following year. Significantly, the basic arguments advanced in these two editorials were devoid of any specific references to Constructivist aims and ideals, although his remarks lamenting the proliferation of "isms" in Soviet art already indicate his concern for the conscious creation of a collective and coherent movement.

Two other articles, published by Ginzburg at this time in the journal *Krasnaia niva*, amplify what in *Style and Epoch* is rather brief and somewhat inadequate commentary on the architecture of the 1923 Moscow Agricultural Exhibition and on the state of modern architecture in the West. In the article reviewing this exhibition, Ginzburg declares his approval of the structures designed by Ivan V. Zholtovsky for their honest expression of the intrinsic nature of wood, which was the prime building material employed throughout the exhibition. As far as Ginzburg was concerned, the distinctive open fretwork of Zholtovsky's main entry to the exhibition—a triumphal arch in timber (pl. 5)—demonstrated that "the language of classical stone triumphal arches has been transposed into wood, but quite straightforwardly, with no desire to deceive, and even with a certain ingenuity that underscores the basic idea (deliberately thin columns, etc.)."[19] It becomes apparent that Ginzburg regarded Zholtovsky's approach to the design of his pavilions and particularly his triumphal arch to be "constructive" in the generic sense, unlike the sham construction evident in recent European and American expositions. It is not a judgment, one suspects, that Ginzburg would have made later in the decade, once his views had hardened into a firm dogma.

The structures which Ginzburg found the most expressive of modern design tendencies were Vladimir Shchuko's Foreign Department Building (pl. 6), Konstantin Melnikov's Makhorka Pavilion (pls. 18,19), and Alexandra Exter and Boris Gladkov's Izvestia Pavilion (pl. 39), all of which pointed the way to a new formal vocabulary. The highlight of Shchuko's building was "its fine bold stairway and large, bright banners over the propylaeum, resounding with purely modern voices."[20] Melnikov's striking pavilion stood out as the "freshest, most original idea, organically interpreted in wood." It was distinguished, in Ginzburg's view, by its utilizing "in a very expedient, interesting, and unquestionably modern way the formal elements of American 'silos.'"[21] That Ginzburg should have pointed to the link between the utilitarian shed-roof form of Melnikov's building and the grain elevators of rural America doubtless reflects his own interest in these structures as paradigms of modern form, a subject which he had previously written about in his first editorial in *Arkhitektura*.[22]

An intriguing facet of Ginzburg's article in *Krasnaia niva* involves his assessment of the pavilions erected by the Union republics at the exhibition. These pavilions, none of which are illustrated in *Style and Epoch*, were found by Ginzburg to be uniformly lackluster and disappointing. This judgment did not stem from their lack of straightforwardness and modernity but rather from the fact that the buildings were poorly sited and that their forms insufficiently exploited the distinctive attributes of their respective regional traditions. The result would have been far more satisfying, Ginzburg maintained, had these pavilions "created their own independent corner, where, organized around the picturesque enclosed square and combined according to their stylistic affinities, they would have presented a glittering, fragrant bouquet of these small but charming cultures."[23] But if this article implied the desirability of assimilating regional aspects into architecture, *Style and Epoch* proceeded to advance a diametrically opposite point of view; "local and national characteristics appear too insignificant," Ginzburg proclaimed here, "when compared with the equaliz-

19. G[inzburg], "Vystavka i arkhitektura" [The Exhibition and Architecture], *Krasnaia niva*, no. 38 (1923), p. 18.
20. Ibid.
21. Ibid., p. 19.
22. Ginzburg's great interest in these structures no doubt was at least partially inspired by Le Corbusier's lead-off article in *L'Esprit Nouveau*, with its seven accompanying illustrations expressing enthusiasm for the aesthetics of American grain elevators; see Le Corbusier-Saugnier, "Trois rappels à MM. les Architectes," in *L'Esprit Nouveau*, no. 1 (n. d.), pp. 90-95. This article appeared as the second chapter in *Vers une architecture*. The subject of Le Corbusier's influence on Ginzburg in this and related connections is discussed below.
23. G[inzburg], "Vystavka i arkhitektura," p. 19.

24. Ginzburg, "Natsional 'naia arkhitektura narodov SSSR" [The National Architecture of the Peoples of the USSR], *S.A.*, nos. 5-6 (1926), pp. 113-14. The article argued that the universal standards made possible by mass production and industrialized building techniques served to obviate the incorporation of traditional stylistic aspects in modern architecture. These standards, coupled with present-day building patterns and requirements and with climatic conditions in a given region, constituted the only valid determinants of a region's or nation's modern architectural form.

25. Ginzburg, "Sovremennaia grazhdanskaia arkhitektura v zapadnoi Evrope" [Modern Civil Architecture in Western Europe], *Krasnaia niva*, no. 22 (1924), p. 531.

ing force of modern technology and economics." This pronounced shift in orientation, reflecting the attitude prevailing in the Modern Movement as a whole, was subsequently reaffirmed by Ginzburg in an article of 1926.[24]

In the second of the two articles written for *Krasnaia niva*, published in 1924, Ginzburg assesses current trends in modern Western architecture. His assessment here serves to augment certain passages in *Style and Epoch*. While German architecture receives the brunt of his criticism, as in the book, a number of appreciative remarks modify the censure which is so unmediated in the longer work. After lamenting Germany's continuing failure to free itself from the shackles of classical influence, he commends its Art Nouveau for having proved "a very healthy, but, alas, unsuccessful attempt to become liberated from these tendencies."[25] This oblique praise of the Art Nouveau is in striking contrast to his sweeping condemnation of the mode in *Style and Epoch*. While in the article he also criticizes current trends in Germany for "glorifying the might and power that have abounded in militant Germany," he nonetheless commends the efforts of some to delete superfluous classical details in order to achieve a heightened articulation of form. Although no architects are named throughout, one suspects that Ginzburg's main referent here is the work of Peter Behrens.

English and French developments also are weighed by Ginzburg. He dismisses the English preoccupation with traditional cottages, much as he does in *Style and Epoch*, censuring such designs for their monotonous repetition of the "now familiar images of a little individual comfort and convenience"; on the other hand, in *Style and Epoch* he was to acknowledge tacitly the collectivizing tendencies inherent in the Garden City movement. His references to developments in French architecture, however, are among the most revealing; disturbed by the apparent dichotomy between the ostentatious splendor of French academic architecture and the austere pioneering developments that gave rise to ferroconcrete and metal constructions like the Eiffel Tower, Ginzburg pointed to Le Corbusier as a kind of conceptual synthesis of the two extremes, finding his articles in *L'Esprit Nouveau* and his book *Vers une architecture* to be the harbingers of an emerging rational spirit in French architecture.

The Principal Themes of *Style and Epoch*

The fundamental arguments underlying Ginzburg's treatise are developed in what are essentially two discrete but interrelated sections of the book. The first consists of the first two chapters and the first portion of the third. This section basically contains an elaboration of the historical rationale which is used to justify Ginzburg's concept of stylistic change and, as a consequence, his theory of modern style. The second section, to which the remainder of the book is devoted, deals with the scope of the methodological problems encountered in adopting a "constructive" approach to modern architecture. The first section is more or less a self-contained discourse on stylistic theory, while the second represents the essence of Ginzburg's position on the creation of a "constructive" architecture.

Although Ginzburg's expansive display of historical erudition sometimes seems to distract from the cogency of his theoretical argument, this part of his analysis nonetheless provides a critical basis for the latter, since it provides examples of those aspects of cumulative architectural and cultural experience which can serve for the construction of a dialectical rationale and method for the evolving modern style. It also serves to demonstrate, as Ginzburg argues, that the evolution of a new architecture must involve a conceptual overcoming and "genetic" recycling of history.

Ginzburg's elaborate dialectical analysis of the great styles in Western architecture is predicated on his argument that this accumulated architectural experience was conditioned by a centuries-old cycle oscillating between the "Greco-Italic" or Greco-Roman classical system—subsequently rearticulated in the Renaissance (thesis)—and its opposite, the Gothic—aspects of which were rearticulated in the Baroque (antithesis). As this cycle was now fully spent, the only genetically viable path for modern architecture inevitably lay beyond it (synthesis). However, given that stylistic change came about through a "genetic" process, it necessarily entailed not the abolition of past systems of creativity, but an assimilation of their seminal principles (law of continuity), which were then integrated with fresh operating concepts and techniques embodying the most significant characteristics of the contemporary epoch (law of independence). Thus, according to Ginzburg's scheme, the principles having "genetic" value for modern architecture, i.e., those capable of engendering something viably new, were those encompassing a synthesis of the organizational methods of Greco-Roman and Renaissance architecture on the one hand, and Gothic and Baroque architecture on the other. He dismissed developments after the Baroque, presumably for their failure to have made any significant theoretical contributions.

Central to Ginzburg's theory of stylistic change is the argument that all great historical styles have been conditioned by the essential factors of their epoch, the particular attributes of their environment, and the material and cultural contingencies of their overall context. Moreover, the distinguishing qualities of great styles are manifested not only in the various prevailing forms of art, but in other contemporaneous forms of human endeavor as well. Each style is perceived to be a self-contained organism that passes through a regular and predictable life cycle consisting of three stages of "genetic" growth: *youth*, which is fundamentally constructive in nature; *maturity*, which is organic; and *old age*, the withering away of a style, which is decorative. The first or constructive stage involves the invention of new building techniques and types that are devoid of decorative embellishment; these arise to accommodate the new societal processes and demands generated by the same factors giving rise to the new style. In the second or organic stage, the perfecting of building type and organic form represents a fulfillment of both utilitarian and aesthetic demands. At this stage constructive and decorative impulses are balanced in an organic unity. Finally, in the third or decorative stage, a straining for effect through overdecoration leads to a gradual erosion of the constructive moment and thus to the progressive withering away of the style.

For Ginzburg, then, a style blossoms from the precisely definable landscape of its own epoch, flourishes, and dies away when it has exhausted all its possibilities. It can never recur in the organic fullness of its original manifestation. Hence, he argues, it is impossible to speak of "progress" in art in anything but the most narrowly technical sense, as each style is a unique expression of the cultural and aesthetic values peculiar to its epoch alone. In the successive development of styles, however, it is eminently possible to discern a discrete evolutionary process at work, one revealing a distinct pattern of growth and an augmentation of the theoretical content that serves to rationalize the form of expression.

The deterministic slant of Ginzburg's genetic concept of stylistic change, viewing each style as if it were a natural organism endowed with a significant life of its own, does not differ appreciably from the basic Darwinian assumption that

19

those forms which survive are the ones best adapted to the environment. To be sure, the Darwinian scientist believes that the characteristics which enable an organism to survive are selected by nature through its own laws, whereas for Ginzburg it is the artist who effectively makes the selection, creating "living," "vital," "viable" forms on the basis of what he considers to be natural or legitimate. Although the "life" of a style may thus be more metaphorical than actual, its existence is nonetheless objectively real and significant, for the ideas and artifacts manifesting style are organic outgrowths of the particular environment—cultural, social, technical—of a given epoch, culture, and society. A corollary to Ginzburg's genetic theory is that a change in style perforce indicates, in addition to the emergence of new aesthetic ideals, a change in the socio-economic make-up of the consumers of architecture and cultural artifacts. Following the basic Marxist argument, the rise of a particular social class with new artistic interests and needs is historically accompanied by, and at times actively induces, major changes in style.

According to Ginzburg, the historical determinants of the new style—the factors unleashing the vital "spark of creative energy" needed to impel the genetic cycle of stylistic change toward a new "constructive" stage and hence a new style—were the Industrial and Russian revolutions. The Industrial Revolution gave rise to the machine, which mechanized the productive forces of society and thereby supplied the scientific and technological base for modern architecture. The Russian Revolution, for its part, advanced the proletariat as the vanguard of a new socio-economic order. As the dominant new group of consumers, the proletariat projected human labor as the prime content of the new society, the unifying symbol of its existence. This, in turn, propelled to the forefront of the new society's architectural concerns the task of solving "all the architectural organisms associated with the concept of labor—*workers' housing* and *the house of work*," the latter encompassing the factory and work place. Given that workers' housing and the factory were destined to be the prime symbols of the new revolutionary epoch—as the temple had been for ancient Greece, the cathedral for the Gothic world, and the palace for the Renaissance—the elements generated by the solution of these two building types had to become the decisive elements of the new style.

2. The Concept of Movement

Ginzburg's notion of style is closely bound up with his concept of movement. Only through a comprehension of movement in architecture, he argues, can the meaning of an architectural work, the articulation and organization of its elements, be fully revealed. That it is at all possible to speak of orderly organization in works of architecture is due to the presence of purely rhythmic aspects which, as palpable manifestations of movement, provide the key to deciphering a particular compositional method. As in *Rhythm in Architecture*, so in *Style and Epoch* Ginzburg is concerned with explaining the nature of movement and its manifestations and consequences in architecture, occasionally resorting to the graphic device of vector diagrams (see chapter 4); his object is to trace the changing historical conceptions of form and expressive values through changing notions of movement. Thus he contrasts the ancient Greek conception of movement, predicated on the classical view of the earth as something reposing in itself and forever forming an immovable center of the cosmos, with that of the Gothic period, which believed the world to be set in motion by a spiritual act of will. The Greek temple, symbolizing forces in static equilibrium, in which neither verticals nor horizontals dominate, is thus opposed by the soaring verticality of the Gothic cathedral, in which there is a dynamic equilibrium of forces. Whereas the Greek temple appears as the embodiment of cosmic repose, the Gothic cathedral looms as a symbol of everlasting change, of movement. In the ensuing genetic cycle of stylistic change and development, the Renaissance is seen by Ginzburg as representing an adaptation of the classical paradigm of architectural form, while the Baroque essentially represents an augmentation and elaboration of the dynamic impulses that had impelled the Gothic.

The third and ultimate category of movement advanced by Ginzburg, supplementing the two preceding systems, is the one made possible by the evolution of the machine, which is "permeated with the genuine rhythm of modernity." The mechanization of production transformed man's understanding of the phenomenal world, whose essence was increasingly perceived as motion-process, with matter being set into motion by the machine. Ginzburg's elucidation of the aesthetic implications of mechanized movement is aimed at suggesting how the machine translates the form of movement into an object of expression, opening up new possibilities for formal articulation and new expressive values capable of extending and supplanting earlier modes of architectural composition.

According to Ginzburg, the form of mechanized movement is determined by the specific dynamics of a machine's performance, by how its productive motion is achieved and sustained. The resulting form of movement literally becomes the prime mover of a dynamic, purposeful composition. The composition of any machine—a crane, a locomotive, or an automobile, for example—is a function not only of a particular type of movement, but also of its direction. Obviously the entire axis of this movement cannot be contained within the bounds of the machine, but extends beyond it as a vector of the machine's projected forward motion. This fact introduces an unprecedented sense of tension and intensity into the resulting asymmetrical composition.

The form and sense of dynamic movement which thus derive from the machine as well as the various industrial and engineering structures are presented by Ginzburg as paradigms for a dynamic and purposefully asymmetrical modern architectural form. Such a form may be wholly asymmetrical, or it may include symmetrical parts arranged in an overall asymmetrical composition. In either case, for Ginzburg the resulting architecture symbolizes "a previously unknown tension of monumental movement." An elevation and analytical diagram of the Vesnin brothers' Palace of Labor competition project are included by Ginzburg in the text (chapter 4) to illustrate the asymmetrical play of compositional forces characteristic of this particular conception of modern architectural form.[26]

As viewed by Ginzburg, mechanization is the end product of a rationalistic view of the world as existing within temporal limits and inclined toward a specific organizational goal and purpose. The mechanization of production, which engendered the essential factors of the modern epoch, and in turn gave rise to the new style, entails the rational subdivision of the process of work into its constituent parts. As the absolute paradigm of rational organization, the machine is designed to perform a specific function and tolerates no "flights of fancy." All its elements have a definite, clear-cut task, one integrated into the overall scheme with absolute precision in order to assure an efficient operation and an effective product.

As it influences other realms of human activity, so the machine can influence art, guiding the artist toward clarity and precision in formulating his creative concepts, which should embody "that ideal of harmonious activity which long ago was formulated by the first Italian theoretician, Alberti." This does not mean

26. Ginzburg's concept of "mechanized movement" bears a certain affinity to the concept of dynamic spatial form devised by the Rationalist movement, the other major avant-garde tendency in Soviet architecture. Although the Rationalists derived their concept from elements of modern art (found in Cubism, Suprematism, the Prouns) and perceptual psychology (Hugo Münsterberg) rather than from the compositional dynamics of the machine, they also regarded the visual tension resulting from asymmetry to be a prime means of energizing form. See my "Aspects of Spatial Form and Perceptual Psychology in the Doctrine of the Rationalist Movement in Soviet Architecture in the 1920s," *VIA 6* (Journal of the Graduate School of Fine Arts, University of Pennsylvania). In press.

3. The Concept of Mechanization

that the machine will replace art, Ginzburg argues. Rather, as the prime symbol of the industrial age and the central fact of life in the emerging proletarian epoch, its influence upon the new artist as well as the mass consumer will determine their concept of what is modern and beautiful.

4. The Concept of Construction

As postulated by Ginzburg, the concept of construction assumes the force of an operational norm and is endowed with a sense of historical and technical inevitability. Conceived as a methodological synthesis of concept, material, and technique, it encompasses not only the material and technical organization of elements in the construction process, but also the intellectual organization of elements within the design process. Although in accord with the basic notion of construction previously advanced by the Constructivists in art, it is sharply redefined to relate expressly to architecture. Thus, the "constructive sensibility," which is seen to endow the architect's working method with its specific character, is derived from the empirical methods of the engineer and constructor, and is thereby distinguished from that of the sculptor and other artists.

It is this concept of construction that underlies Ginzburg's idea of a "constructive" architecture, as well as his positivist aesthetic of the "new style." It is vital to realize, however, that for Ginzburg "constructivism" does not constitute a particular formal style. A "constructivist" architecture embodies the means to style but not style itself, a working method for designing an organic "constructive" form but not a preconceived idea of its appearance. That which is "constructivist" in Ginzburg's scheme, then, is not style but *method*.

Theoretical Influences on Ginzburg

As has already been noted, Ginzburg was deeply immersed in architectural history and aesthetic theory at this point in his career. Given his classical training, there are probably few major sources in these fields that he did not consult and to whom he was not in some way indebted. To say that he was a true eclectic in his theorizing is not to suggest, however, that he was merely the mouthpiece for the views of others. Though not all of his thoughts are original, he had an impressive capacity to synthesize a disparate array of sources and ideas into an intellectually fresh and coherent construct.

1. Stylistic Change and Related Theories

27. The following discussion focuses only on those aesthetic theories of stylistic change which exerted the most immediate influence on Ginzburg's own construct in *Style and Epoch*. Yet these theories obviously are variously indebted to earlier conceptions. The most notable of these in the context of Ginzburg's concerns is that of the *Kunstwollen* (the "will to form" or the "aesthetic impulse" of a particular culture or epoch), promulgated by Alois Riegl (1858–1905) in his *Stilfragen* (Berlin: G. Siemens, 1893) and *Die Spätrömische Kunstindustrie* (Vienna: K. K. Hof, 1901). Manifested equally in the fine and the minor arts, Riegl's *Kunstwollen* concept focuses on

Ginzburg drew heavily on the ideas of Heinrich Wölfflin, Paul Frankl, and Oswald Spengler for his theory of stylistic change. The extreme determinism of Spengler and Georgi Plekhanov provided vital material on the subject of causes, while Wölfflin, Frankl, and Spengler illuminated the determining power of early patterns.[27]

Wölfflin's work was widely influential in Russia at the turn of the century. The translation of his three major books prior to the revolution was accompanied by the acceptance of the "science of art" method (*Kunstwissenschaft*) as the preferred approach to the study of artistic phenomena. That method resurfaced in the early twenties to become the leading mode of Soviet art criticism.[28] Wölfflin's approach offered Ginzburg a conceptual framework for examining the larger sequences of art history in terms of attributes that were not pure abstractions but derived from observation, thus providing the structure for treating concrete subject matter in art. Wölfflin's statement, "Study the epoch and you will comprehend its style," supplied not only a fundamental rationale, but perhaps even the title for Ginzburg's treatise.[29] This statement epitomizes the basic Wölfflinian *Zeitgeist* argument wholly embraced by Ginzburg—that styles are the direct expression of the temperament of a time and people.

Wölfflin posited a theory of development to account for the parallels among the visual arts in any circumscribed period, as well as for the alternation of distinctive characteristics from one period to another. He used the set of five pairs of contrasting concepts he had initially devised to describe the evolution from Renaissance to Baroque (linearity to painterliness, plane to recession, closed to open form, multiplicity to unity, absolute to relative clarity) to explain the development of style within any period of Western art and to illuminate the transition from one style to another. These transitions, which were of particular interest to Ginzburg, were perceived to be not linear but spiral: the regeneration of a style did not return it to its initial point of departure, but subjected it to an entirely new synthesis, thereby making it a springboard for the ensuing new style.

While Ginzburg appropriated Wölfflin's construct as the basic structure for his own scheme, he drew numerous supplementary elements from other sources as well. The laws of continuity and independence, which he conceived as polar opposites propelling the evolution and the change of a style, respectively, bear a striking resemblance to those of "tradition" and "originality" advanced by Paul Frankl as the cornerstone of his concept of stylistic development in *Entwicklungsphasen der neueren Baukunst*.[30] Although overshadowed by Wölfflin's popularity, Frankl's work was known in Russia through an art historian known personally by Ginzburg, Alexander G. Gabrichevsky, who had studied with Frankl in Munich.[31] According to Frankl, tradition, which provided a common source of forms, was the prime element of continuity linking the four phases of post-medieval architecture that were the objects of his study; originality, or the desire to "accomplish something better than before, that is, to fulfill what was left unfulfilled by the previous performance," distinguished one phase from the next.[32] An interaction between tradition and originality occurred in all artistic activity, he affirmed, as genuine creativity was impossible without the effect of both. This was to be Ginzburg's argument as well. Another of Frankl's concepts that finds reflection in Ginzburg's framework is that of "purposive intention" (*Zweckgesinnung*)—the relationship of buildings to the social institutions for which they are conceived—as a vital factor of stylistic evolution. This emphasis on social function, augmenting Wölfflin's *Zeitgeist* theory of style, was subsequently given a more overtly Marxist interpretation in Ginzburg's analytical framework.

Although Wölfflin's and Frankl's constructs thus combined to offer a compelling general description of immanent style-forces, their explanations of the causes for periodic changes in style were predicated on nothing more than a vague determinism. A more decisive explanation of that process, as well as of other themes developed in *Style and Epoch*, was supplied by Oswald Spengler's *Untergang des Abendlandes*.[33] Although departing sharply from the Wölfflin-Frankl methodological framework, Spengler's overall conceptions were still sufficiently complementary in intent to lend themselves to an ingenious conceptual synthesis in Ginzburg's own construct.

Like Wölfflin and Frankl, Spengler rejected linear progression, believing that evolution represented the fulfillment of form. According to his "morphological" method—which like Ginzburg's genetic method basically adapted the Darwinian concept of living forms to explain historical development—cultures were self-contained organisms going through prescribed stages of birth, growth, matur-

the larger set of interrelated formal attributes and principles characterizing a historical period rather than on the intentions of the individual artist. To comprehend the *Kunstwollen* of a particular epoch requires viewing stylistic phenomena genetically, or reconstructing their lineage from their ancestry through their subsequent manifestations. For Riegl, then, changes in style are manifestations of a replacement of one set of aesthetic ideals by another, or of changes in the *Kunstwollen* embodying these ideals. Riegl's concept of the *Kunstwollen* bears a certain affinity to Hegel's idea of the *Zeitgeist*, which permeated virtually all later German aesthetic thought, including that of Gottfried Semper, Riegl, Wölfflin, Frankl, Wilhelm Worringer, and Spengler.

28. B. B. Mikhailov, "O nekotorykh metodologicheskikh poiskakh sovetskogo iskusstvoznaniia" [Regarding Certain Methodological Pursuits in Soviet Art Criticism], *Sovetskoe iskusstvoznanie '75* (Moscow, 1976), pp. 283-85. See also A. A. Sidorov, "Iskusstvoznanie za 10 let v SSSR" [Art Criticism in the USSR Over the Past Ten Years], *Trudy sektsii iskusstvoznaniia*. Institut arkheologii i iskusstvoznaniia, vol. 2 (Moscow, 1928), pp. 5-15. Wölfflin's *Die klassische Kunst* (1899) was translated as *Klassicheskoe iskusstvo*, trans. A. A. Konstantinova and V. M. Nevezhina (St. Petersburg: Brokgauz-Effron, 1912); his *Renaissance und Barock* (1888), as *Renessans i barokko*, trans. E. Lunberg (St. Petersburg: Griadushchii den', 1913); his *Kunstgeschichtliche Grundbegriffe* (1915), as *Istolkovanie iskusstva*, trans. and intro. by B. Vipper (Moscow: Del'fin, 1922).

29. Heinrich Wölfflin, *Istolkovanie iskusstva*, p. 20; quoted in book review by Nikolai Tarabukin in *Pechat' i revoliutsiia*, no. 7 (1922), p. 341.

30. Paul Frankl, *Die Entwicklungsphasen der neueren Baukunst* (Leipzig: Teubner, 1914); Eng. trans.: *Principles of Architectural History*, trans. and ed. James F. O'Gorman (Cambridge, Mass.: MIT Press, 1968).

31. V. F. Markuzon, "Aleksandr Georgievich Gabrichevsky (1891-1968)," *Sovetskoe iskusstvo '76* (Moscow, 1976), pp. 346-47.

32. Frankl, *Principles of Architectural History*, p. 192.

33. Oswald Spengler, *Der Untergang des Abendlandes* (Munich: C. H. Beck'sche, 1918); Eng. trans.: *The Decline of the West*, trans. C. F. Atkinson (2 vols.; New

York: Knopf, 1926–1928). The first volume was translated into Russian as *Zakat Evropy* [The Decline of Europe], trans. L. D. Frenkel (Moscow-Petrograd: Mospoligraf, 1923). Spengler's book had prophesied that Russia would be the savior of the world following the decline of Western (or "Faustian") culture, and that it was thus destined to develop a new "great style" of architecture based on a new religion or ideology. While Ginzburg remarks on the prospect of arriving at "our 'great style,'" this prophecy alone hardly demonstrates the full extent of Spengler's appeal for Ginzburg. Interestingly, Spengler's aesthetic views precipitated the publication in 1922 of a pithy book by the later distinguished art historian Victor N. Lazarev, *Osval'd Shpengler i ego vzgliady na iskusstvo* [Oswald Spengler and His Views on Art] (Moscow: A. G. Mironov, 1922). Dismissing Spengler's cyclical theory of history as unhistorical nonsense, Lazarev argued that Spengler's work nonetheless possessed great value by virtue of its having rendered integral portraits of whole cultures, demonstrating that all forms of creative endeavor in a culture speak with one language. Not least, Spengler had succeeded in embodying the many ideas in the air in recent years in a statement that pointed to a new direction in which European aesthetic thought could develop, "if this is what the genius artist desires" (p. 152). Ginzburg appears to have taken up the challenge. Constructivist art critic and theoretician Nikolai Tarabukin also found Spengler's ideas on art extraordinarily representative of the time, drawing on them to support some of his arguments in *Ot mol'berta k mashine* [From the Easel to the Machine], to be discussed below.

34. Spengler, *The Decline of the West*, vol. 1, p. 222.

35. Worringer, *Abstraktion und Einfühlung* (Munich: R. Piper, 1908; Eng. trans. M. Bullock, Cleveland-New York: World Pub. Co., 1967). Although a student of Wölfflin, Worringer emerged in his treatise as a disciple of Riegl and Theodor Lipps. Worringer's concept of *Weltgefühl* was derived from Riegl's *Kunstwollen;* his point of departure is Lipps's theory of *Einfühlung* (Empathy), the reverse of abstraction in man's perception of form.

36. In his treatise, Worringer contrasts the "Cisalpine" art of Southern man with the "Transalpine" art of Northern man. The notion of such a north-south polarity had earlier been broached by Riegl.

37. Spengler, *Decline*, vol. 1, p. 177.

ity, and decay—or spring, summer, autumn, and winter. A culture thus was born out of a decisive and concrete set of circumstances and died when it had exhausted all its possibilities. Each culture had its own innate "great style," one which embodied its own unique set of circumstances in art and in all other realms of creative endeavor, from physics and mathematics to morals and politics. Its forms proceeded through an identical life cycle: in the springtime of a style—Ginzburg's organic or constructive phase—"architecture is lord and ornament is vassal"; as the style developed, ornament gradually came into ascendancy until, in the final period of decline, ornament gave way to imitation. Western art and architecture, Spengler argued, had suffered such a decline since the nineteenth century, and their possibilities were fully exhausted.

"What the creation of a masterpiece means for an individual artist," Spengler wrote, "the creation of a *species* of art, comprehended as such, means for the life history of a culture. It is epochal."[34] In Spengler's framework Ginzburg found a compelling paradigm for interpreting the underlying causes and dynamics of stylistic change, as well as ultimately for determining the specific aspects of the new style. Borrowing from Wilhelm Worringer's belief that every style was the product of the "world-feeling" (*Weltgefühl*) of the age that had created it,[35] Spengler argued that each culture and its great style were marked by certain basic attributes, or prime symbols, which permeated all of life and thought. Properly defined and understood, they provided the key to understanding the history and character of the culture as a whole and its corresponding style. This belief underlies Ginzburg's own that the machine, mechanized production, and labor were the prime symbols of his epoch and hence destined to be the prime determinants of the new style.

Other Spenglerian arguments, removed from their original context in Spengler's problematic cyclical theory of history, also contribute to Ginzburg's interpretation of historical developments. In his theory, Spengler had reconstituted the traditional succession of ancient, medieval, and modern historical periods into six great independent cultures. Of these, the classical, or "Apollinian," culture encompassed the civilizations of Greece and Rome, while the medieval and modern periods made up the "Faustian" culture comprising modern Western society. The opposition which Spengler established at various levels between the two is echoed in *Style and Epoch*. Ginzburg employs the same contrast, which had also been suggested by Worringer,[36] between the rational ideal of Greek art as the embodiment of Southern man and the impulsive brilliance of the Gothic as embodying Northern man. Also surfacing in Ginzburg's analysis is Spengler's contrasting of the static space of Greek architecture with the "pure and limitless space" of the Gothic. Spengler's assertion that the Greek space "hovers" while the Gothic "soars," revealing dynamic principles of "straining movement, force, and mass,"[37] closely accords with Ginzburg's analysis of their respective implications in terms of space and movement. There is little reason to doubt that Ginzburg's view of the importance of the Gothic was influenced as much by Spengler's treatment, which had in turn been drawn from Worringer's interpretation of the style,[38] as by that of Viollet-le-Duc, whose influence nonetheless cannot be discounted.[39] Spengler's contention that Baroque space, with its "passion for the third dimension," achieved the ultimate level of dynamic articulation likewise seems to underlie Ginzburg's reference to the Baroque as the last great style.

While the theories of Wölfflin, Frankl, and Spengler provided Ginzburg with much of his framework for describing the nature of stylistic change, they did little to explain the forces producing that change. In seeking that explanation, Ginzburg obviously turned to Plekhanov. The first Marxist to devote substantial attention to investigating a wide range of artistic subjects, Georgi V. Plekhanov was in Ginzburg's day the only plausible source for a coherent Marxist aesthetic. His writings on the subject, which applied the deterministic aspect of Marxism to the genesis of art and art forms, had supplied the fundamental Marxist texts on art in pre-revolutionary Russia. His authority was revived after the revolution with the publication in 1922 of a collection of his essays on art, in which he was praised as the father of Marxist aesthetics.[40] Central to Plekhanov's view was the concept that art arises as a virtually automatic process from the movement of history, called into being by the needs of the class or stratum whose tastes it expresses. That concept accords fully with Ginzburg's premise that the emergence of a new style accompanies the rise of a new social group destined to become the prime consumers of art. Further coinciding with Ginzburg's argument is Plekhanov's notion that there are moments in the evolution of each art form when unexploited and latent potentialities suddenly emerge into view, to be assimilated by those artists who can grasp their implications. Significantly, it was Plekhanov who was chiefly responsible for the incorporation into Marxism of Karl Bücher's theory, propounded in his *Arbeit und Rhythmus* (1897), linking the creation of art to the labor process, especially in primitive art.[41] Ginzburg had earlier drawn on Bücher in *Rhythm in Architecture* for his argument that rhythm both animates and embodies societal processes.

Also striking is the extent to which Ginzburg's approach to devising a historical rationale for stylistic change and ultimately for the new style reflects the premises underlying Plekhanov's concept of "scientific aesthetics." According to Plekhanov, scientific aesthetics sought not to prescribe style, but rather to discern how the different laws and modes of expression prevailing in different epochs had evolved and to investigate those laws accounting for art's historical development. Plekhanov, being strongly influenced by Darwin, likewise relied on evolutionary thought to support his argument that the origin and character of aesthetic feelings were rooted in the fundamentals of biology, as was the genesis of formal development. Although Spengler made more explicit use of the organic or Darwinian metaphor in his analysis of artistic forms and evolution, Plekhanov's Darwinian rationale allowed him to define a "utilitarian" art as an art vitally useful in sustaining man's struggle for life. This concept became fundamental in Ginzburg's argument.

The sources on which Ginzburg drew in order to establish the historical determinants of stylistic change could offer him little help in rationalizing the appearance of the "new" style, beyond making clear that the determinants had to be sought in the circumstances of the epoch. Insights into the specific nature of these circumstances had to be found elsewhere. Indeed, Wölfflin had insisted that technical factors were incapable of creating a style, arguing that the word "art" implied a particular conception of form which technical expediency could not be permitted to contradict.[42] Similarly, although Spengler recognized the growing power of the machine and its "priest" the engineer, he had little of significance to say about the mechanization process, which he personally abhorred.[43]

The most obvious, though not necessarily the most profound, influence on Ginzburg's formulation of a full-fledged "machine aesthetic" was that of Le Corbusier's early writings on architecture. It is doubtful that the initial, 1923 edition of *Vers une architecture* could have reached Ginzburg before he wrote his own

38. The polarity between the Greek temple and the Gothic cathedral, first postulated by Worringer in his treatise, was amplified in his *Formproblem der Gotik* (Munich: R. Piper, 1911; Eng. trans. Herbert Read, London: G. P. Putnam's Sons, 1927).

39. Ginzburg would have surely known Viollet-le-Duc's *Entretiens sur l'architecture* (2 vols.; Paris: A. Morel, 1863–1872; first Rus. trans. 1937–1938). Both men were vitally concerned with the question of style. According to Viollet, style resided in the rational expression of an idea, not in the visual aspects of form. Inherent in all arts of an epoch, style evolved through infancy, maturity, decline, and old age. Viollet thus believed that a modern style would emerge not from reviving past styles, but from rationally adapting their underlying principles to modern times. Aspects of such a style were already evident in the naval and railway architecture of his day, in which the "constructeurs de machines" directly expressed modern needs (*Entretiens*, I, p. 186); here, perhaps, is the source of Ginzburg's reference to the constructor of the machine. Complicating the issue of Viollet's influence is his provocative *L'Art russe* (Paris: A. Morel, 1877; Rus. trans. N. V. Sultanov, Moscow, 1879). By summoning Russian architects to revive the spirit of seventeenth-century Muscovite architecture, Viollet's book bolstered the nationalist program in Russian architecture. See E. I. Kirichenko, "Problema natsional'nogo stilia v arkhitekture Rossii 70-kh gg. XIX v." [Problems of a National Style in Russian Architecture in the 1870s], *Arkhitekturnoe nasledtsvo*, vol. 25 (1976), pp. 131-53.

2. The Mechanical Analogy and Le Corbusier

40. *G. V. Plekhanov i iskusstvo* [G. V. Plekhanov and Art]. Intro. by L. Akselrod and by V. Friche (Moscow: Novaia Moskva, 1922). Friche's essay is republ. as "G. V. Plekhanov i 'Nauchnaia estetika'" [G. V. Plekhanov and "Scientific Aesthetics"] in his compendium *Problemy iskusstvovedeniia* (Moscow: Gosizdat, 1930), pp. 5-19.

41. Bücher, *Arbeit und Rhythmus* (Leipzig: B. G. Teubner, 1897). Bücher (1847–1930) was a German economist and economic historian whose leading work, *Die Entstehung der Volkswirtschaft* (Tübingen: H. Laupp, 1898), proposed a three-phase scheme of preindustrial development encompassing "household," "town," and "national" economies. His *Arbeit und Rhythmus* is indicative of the breadth of his interests: focusing on the relation between the physiology and the psychology of labor, this treatise sets out his theory of the origin of the arts in the rhythmical movements of collective labor. According to Bücher, labor among primitive peoples approaches play in both form and substance. The most intriguing aspect of the treatise is his argument that all regularly sustained activity finally takes on a rhythmic form and becomes fused with music and song in an indivisible whole. Bücher's assertion that play is older than labor and art is older than the production of useful objects haunted Plekhanov, who saw in it a possible refutation of historical materialism. Plekhanov came to grips with this theory in his essay "Labor, Play, and Art" (from his *Letter Without Address No. 3*). In it, he cites Herbert Spencer to affirm that the content of play in primitive cultures is determined by such activity as assists in the support of their existence.

42. Wölfflin, *Renaissance and Baroque*, trans. Kathrin Simon (Ithaca, N.Y.: Cornell University Press, 1966), p. 79.

43. In the last chapter of the *Decline*, titled "The Machine," Spengler argued that the machine was a Satanic weapon that tended to enslave the entrepreneur and dominate the earth. The theme of an unceasing struggle between nature and humanity initially sketched out in this chapter was subsequently developed into an explicit theory in Spengler's *Der Mensch und die Technik* (Munich: Beck, 1931; Eng. trans. C. F. Atkinson, New York: Knopf, 1932).

3. Constructivism and Production Art

treatise. However, Le Corbusier's book had previously been published between 1920 and 1922 as a series of essays in *L'Esprit Nouveau*, though not in exactly the same order in which they appear in the book. That this journal had reached Moscow without too much delay is confirmed by the publication in the fall of 1922 of Nikolai Tarabukin's review of its sixteenth issue, which contains the last of the articles comprising *Vers une architecture*.[44]

These articles proclaimed the message that ships, airplanes, automobiles, and grain elevators had certain lessons for the architect, and that the expressiveness and harmony of the Parthenon would most closely correspond in a modern, scientific age to sensations of a mechanical kind. The Greek temple was seen to be related by its apparent formal and constructive standardization to the large machines with which modern man was becoming increasingly familiar as a growing presence in his everyday life. The standards of the machine could teach the architect that a well-stated problem found its solution naturally, and that the standards of that solution could be determined by logical analysis and experimentation.

That such evocations of the mechanical idea had an immediate impact on Ginzburg is apparent from his editorial "The Aesthetics of Modernity," which must have been written shortly after perusing *L'Esprit Nouveau*. The editorial's illustrations of the Buffalo grain elevator, its assertion that the new aesthetic spirit was the spirit of the machine, and its paeans to industrial and engineering structures as paradigms of modern form reveal Ginzburg's unmistakable debt to Le Corbusier. The format of *Style and Epoch*, whose illustrations feature ships, airplanes, factories, engineering structures, and various kinds of mechanized objects in addition to grain elevators, bears an even more direct relationship to that of Le Corbusier's articles, although Ginzburg employs far fewer illustrations and makes little effort to coordinate them with the text.

Beyond these apparent similarities, however, there are significant differences. Ginzburg's historical analysis of architectural developments is more scholarly and comprehensive than Le Corbusier's; the contrast between Le Corbusier's cursory dismissal of the Gothic and Ginzburg's more favorable treatment of it, for example, is indicative of the latter's greater objectivity and concern for historical process. But the ultimate source of the difference between the two stems from their respective perceptions of the relationship between the engineer and the architect. Despite his obvious enthusiasm for the engineer's aesthetic, Le Corbusier ultimately viewed it as distinct from that of the architect; where the engineer might achieve a harmonious form simply by observing the law of economy, the architect's formal expression depended on an order that embodied the Platonic spirit, alone the source of beauty in art. Ginzburg, on the other hand, argues for a fundamental symbiosis of the engineer's and the architect's methods, emphasizing the former as a paradigm for conceptualizing and organizing the latter. Le Corbusier's rhapsodic observations on the machine's implications for architecture are aesthetically inspired but technically naive. In contrast, Ginzburg's complex and sometimes elaborate arguments are grounded in the experience of his polytechnical as well as classical training, making their extrapolation into aesthetic theory more authoritative.

The essential elements of the Constructivist theory of an industrial or "production" art exerted an obvious influence on Ginzburg's thinking. Although he conspicuously refrained from linking his own theory with that of the Constructivist movement in art, the latter's ideology helped define the conceptual parameters of the arguments developed in *Style and Epoch*.

The genesis of the Constructivist idea in Soviet art is traceable to Vladimir Tatlin's complex "counter-reliefs," executed in 1913–1914, which emphasized the use of "real materials in real space." Fundamental to these reliefs was the conceptual shift from the flat canvas of painting to the more "constructive" medium of the three-dimensional object, reflecting not only the intrinsic nature of the materials employed but also the means of combining and supporting them. Tatlin's belief that material dictates technique and that technique, in turn, determines form obtained its ultimate expression in his Monument to the Third International of 1919–1920 (p. 95). Its dynamic, light construction was conceived to exploit the ultimate aesthetic and technical potentials of steel and glass, unified into a dynamic whole by mechanized movement.

The decisive crystallization of a discrete Constructivist aesthetic occurred inside INKHUK, the Institute of Artistic Culture, which elaborated Tatlin's theories by placing ideological emphasis on utilizing industrial techniques to produce utilitarian, socially useful products. Founded in Moscow in 1920 as a center for artistic research, INKHUK emerged as the paramount vehicle for clarifying the emerging tendencies in early Soviet avant-garde art. Following Wassily Kandinsky's brief tenure as president (a term cut short by the rejection of his idiosyncratic program),[45] INKHUK launched a program formulated by the sculptor Aleksei V. Babichev for the "objective analysis" of art in both theoretical and applied (laboratory) realms.[46] The dominant topic of investigation had to do with the formal and technical distinctions between "composition" and "construction." As the initial discussion effectively affirmed Tatlin's earlier conclusion that literal construction was impossible in painting, the focus shifted to defining the nature of construction. The resulting debate, which compelled the participants to particularize their concepts and clarify the differences among themselves, gave rise to the formation in March 1921 of the "First Working Group of Constructivists," which became the initial nucleus of the movement. Although Tatlin's work exerted an obvious influence on the group, he was not one of its members and never became closely associated with the movement as such. Central to the group's position was Varvara Stepanova's declaration that "technology and industry have confronted art with the problem of *construction* not as a contemplative representation, but as an active function."[47]

In November 1921 INKHUK was reorganized under the leadership of Osip Brik, Boris Arvatov, and Nikolai Tarabukin, who brought with them the concept of production art. The majority of INKHUK's members, comprising Constructivists and their supporters, proclaimed their adherence to a new program committed to "the absolute value of industrial art and to Constructivism as its only form of expression."[48] Thus evolved the theoretical program which embraced Productivism, or the concept of an industrialized production art, as the principal means for organizing the material elements of industrialization in a purposeful way in order to produce a utilitarian and socially useful art. The main tenets of *Style and Epoch* clearly are closely affiliated with the basic thesis underlying this program.

This thesis was elaborated through the 1921 "Productivist Manifesto" issued by the INKHUK Constructivists[49] and further amplified in Aleksei Gan's *Konstruktivizm* of 1922, which appeared as a highly polemical synthesis of normative aesthetics and ideology. Tectonics (*tektonika*), facture (*faktura*),[50] and construction (*konstruktsiia*)—each redefined in the new context—were pos-

44. Nikolai Tarabukin, review of *L'Esprit Nouveau*, no. 16, in *Pechat' i revoliutsiia*, no. 7 (Sept.-Oct. 1922), pp. 349-50. Reviews of *Vers une architecture* began to appear in late 1924, indicating that the book had arrived earlier that year; cf. N. Iarovskaia, *Pechat' i revoliutsiia*, no. 5 (Sept.–Oct. 1924), pp. 349-50; and B. A. Korshunov, "O printsipakh arkhitekturnogo stroitel'stva" [Concerning Principles of Architectural Construction], *Stroitel'naia promyshlennost'*, no. 12 (1924), pp. 758-60. Korshunov's review was followed by a commentary by Aleksei V. Shchusev (pp. 760-62), which addressed certain issues raised by Le Corbusier's book without actually referring to or discussing the book itself.

45. Kandinsky's INKHUK program proposed investigating the formal and psychological aspects of modern art. See his "Skhematicheskaia programma rabot Instituta khudozhestvennoi kul'tury po planu V. V. Kandinskogo" [Schematic Program for the Work of the Institute of Artistic Culture According to V. V. Kandinsky's Plan], in *Sovetskoe iskusstvo za 15 let. Materialy i dokumentatsiia*, ed. I. L. Matsa (Moscow-Leningrad: Ogiz-Izogiz, 1933), pp. 126-39. After eight months, Kandinsky's program was rejected in favor of the one devised by Aleksei V. Babichev, and Kandinsky left INKHUK.

46. Babichev's notes on his program are reproduced in Dmitrii V. Sarabianov, *Aleksei Vasil'evich Babichev: khudozhnik, teoretik, pedagog* [Aleksei Vasil'evich Babichev: Artist, Theoretician, Pedagogue] (Moscow: Sovetskii khudozhnik, 1974), p. 104. Babichev's program was used as a point of departure by the Rationalists; cf. my article cited supra, n. 26.

47. Varst [*Varvara Stepanova*], statement accompanying her work, in *5 × 5 = 25. Katalog vystavki* [5 × 5 = 25. Catalogue of the Exhibition] (Moscow, 1921), n. p. The five artists, with five contributions each, represented in the exhibition were, in addition to Stepanova, Alexandra Exter, Alexander Rodchenko, Liubov Popova, and Alexander Vesnin. The exhibition was held in September 1921.

48. Quoted in Victor M. Lobanov, *Khudozhestvennye gruppirovki za poslednie 25 let* [Artistic Groupings over the Past Twenty-five Years] (Moscow: 1930), p. 101.

49. The "Program of the Productivist Group"—as the INKHUK Constructivists called themselves at the time to underscore their commitment to the idea

of a "production" art—was issued in the fall of 1921 over the signatures of Alexander Rodchenko and Varvara Stepanova; a translation of the program appears in *Gabo: Constructions, Sculpture, Painting, Drawing, Engravings* (Cambridge, Mass.: Harvard Univ. Press, 1957).

50. Facture, a word not in common usage in English, is defined by *Webster's New World Dictionary* (2d ed., 1978) as "the manner of making something, especially a work of art." It must be pressed into service here by virtue of being the exact equivalent of the similar Russian word *faktura*. While it has previously been translated as "texture" (cf. the extracts from Gan's *Konstruktivizm* in *Russian Art of the Avant-Garde*, ed. and trans. John E. Bowlt [New York: Viking, 1976], p. 225 and passim), this is not its meaning, as is made clear by Gan himself. He writes in *Konstruktivizm* that by "facture" he and his Constructivist colleagues have in mind "the working of a material in its entirety, from its initial state as raw material to finished product, and *not simply of its surface*" (p. 61, italics mine).

51. References in both documents were to "communism" and not to "socialism." The former word was quickly abandoned, however, especially after the institution of the New Economic Policy, once it was officially determined that the ultimate stage of communism had not yet been reached, and that the current stage was that of socialism, a transitional phase.

52. This triad was first advanced by Aleksei Gan in his *Konstruktivizm*, p. 48.

tulated as the dialectical triad of the program. Tectonics, regarded as the ideological underpinning of constructive art, meant the systematic exploitation of the latest technological resources of material and technique to produce a utilitarian art capable of fulfilling and embodying the principle of communist collectivity.[51] Facture meant the deliberate selection of materials which, on the basis of their intrinsic nature and mode of production, could fulfill the specific requirements of a given problem; emphasis was placed on preserving the inherent quality of the transformed material while at the same time directly expressing the nature of its transformation into the finished product. Construction meant the synthesizing organization of concept, material, and technique to arrive at the most effective fabrication of the projected end product.

Despite its iconoclastic bombast and militancy, Gan's *Konstruktivizm* crystallized certain ideas outlined in embryonic form in the "Productivist Manifesto," making it the first attempt to elaborate the Constructivist ideology. Although Gan did not regard Constructivism purely as a Russian phenomenon, he asserted that only the Soviet Union, having socialized production and society through a proletarian revolution, offered conditions conducive to its ultimate realization.

Gan's treatise, like the Productivist program, called for a revolt against the cult of "pure beauty" and denounced traditional art for being inexorably linked to "theological, metaphysical, and mystical premises" inimical to the emerging communist culture of labor and intellect. Hence the remarkable early Constructivist dictum: "We declare unconditional war on art!" Gan maintained that the only aspects of the past artistic heritage retaining any significance for a communist culture were those skills and accumulated experience derived from the actual production of art.

Although Ginzburg never referred to either Gan's book or the Productivist program by name, his conception essentially accorded with the Constructivist thesis while refuting Gan's negation of aesthetics as a whole. Thus, while Ginzburg agreed with the rejection of metaphysical values as a basis for aesthetic judgment, he also contended that the revolution had not obviated the need for aesthetics, but rather had transformed their fundamental character by setting into motion those factors which had given rise to the new "constructive" moment.

In a short concluding chapter devoted largely to architecture, Gan wrote that architecture was the ultimate manifestation of the Constructivist objective of giving material form to the new way of life and that the new communist city was the paramount setting for its realization. While Gan crystallized the basic elements of the Constructivist ideology, he did so in terms that were too polemical and elementary to find any direct reflection in *Style and Epoch*. It remained chiefly for Tarabukin, Arvatov, and Brik to take his relatively simplistic formulation and rework it into the more explicit triad of "labor, technique, and organization,"[52] which then became the essential interacting principles of the Constructivist concept of an industrialized art.

The professed aim of the industrialized, production-oriented art promulgated by the Constructivists was to organize the material elements of industrial production in a purposive manner. Fundamental to this principle of "expediency," which derived from the implications of mechanized production, was the belief that a socially useful art had a paramount responsibility both to optimize the specific purposes for which it was intended and to satisfy the particular conditions of its production. Subsumed within this principle was a drive to achieve a maximum economy of means in the use and processing of materials; a simplification of form through standardized, mass-produced elements, and finally a maximized effectiveness in both producing a given object and accommodating it to the purpose for which it was intended.

Also central to the idea of production art was the definition of labor in art in terms of material labor. Gan's initial attempt to rationalize the creative act in terms of material labor was amplified and refined by Nikolai Tarabukin in his text *Ot mol'berta k mashine* [From the Easel to the Machine]. Tarabukin, like Gan, maintained that the value of art derived from the work expended in giving material a form which satisfied a particular purpose. He also sought to extend this thesis to encompass the implications of the collective form of labor inherent in industrialized production. Tarabukin redefined the artist's role in terms of the division of labor, which had, of course, already replaced traditional specialization. Instead of the special status traditionally accorded the artist, Tarabukin argued that the artist's role in the modern production process was of the same import as that of the engineer and master craftsman, inasmuch as they were all participants who performed vital and distinct but interdependent roles in the overall process. "The concept of 'the artist in production,'" he wrote, "encompasses both the engineer who guides the general course of production and the master craftsman standing directly beside the machine."[53]

This postulation, which supplied the platform from which the Constructivists urged artists to become involved in production and industrial art, was directed toward demystifying the creative process. The assumption was that it was imperative to replace the subjectivity of taste, chance, and creative inspiration by the empirical methods of the engineer and master craftsman. The engineer's method, embracing the latest scientific principles, would instill the artist with a vital sense of discipline, providing an organizational method for coordinating his work and integrating its end product into the total production process. This thinking, of course, explains the identification of the artist with the engineer in Constructivist theory, a conceptual link which Boris Arvatov characterized as the "problem of professional artistic engineering."[54] At the same time, the connection to the master craftsman, though in a sense appearing to be a throwback to the preindustrial handicraft tradition, was likewise linked to the industrialized production process: it reflected the belief that the craftsman in the pit possessed a unique understanding of the intrinsic nature of industrialized materials and methods as well as of the utilitarian products that they were capable of generating, and that this understanding should be emulated by the artist. Accordingly, the concept of "art as labor" became virtually synonymous with that of "art as craftsmanship" and ultimately "art as technique." This led, in turn, to the notion that *technique*, the means, was to replace *style*, the end, as the operational focus of Constructivist method.

Mention should here be made of Alexander A. Bogdanov, whose concept of a proletarian culture served as a catalyst for certain fundamental Soviet avant-garde attitudes, including those embodied in the Constructivist notion of an industrially based art. Initially, Bogdanov sought to supplement what he believed to be a philosophical gap in Marxism with the epistemological foundations provided by the positivism of Ernst Mach and Richard Avenarius, from which Bogdanov derived the view that all life is pure experience, empirically and scientifically knowable.[55] Bogdanov was the first to promulgate the "collectivist" idea

53. Nikolai M. Tarabukin, *Ot mol'berta k mashine* (Moscow: Rabotnik prosveshcheniia, 1923), p. 32. The central argument of Tarabukin's book involves the need for "the complete dissolution of easel art and . . . the appearance of a new form of production skill" aimed at fulfilling a utilitarian end, one of "creative activism" (p. 35). Tarabukin's book has been translated into French by Andrei B. Nakov and Michel Pétris as *Du chevalet à la machine*, in *Nikolai Taraboukine: Le dernier tableau* (Paris: Champ Libre, 1972), pp. 25-84.

54. Boris Arvatov, in his review of Tarabukin's *Ot mol'berta k mashine*, in *LEF*, no. 4 (Aug.–Dec. 1924), p. 210.

55. Bogdanov also drew on the language theories of Max Müller and the monism of German biologist Ernst Haeckel. Bogdanov was the leading figure of the group of pre-revolutionary Russian intellectuals known as the Empiriocritics. The positivist philosophy of Empiriocriticism embraced by Bogdanov, Anatoli V. Lunacharsky, and others of this group had first been promulgated by Richard Avenarius and the Austrian physicist-philosopher Ernst Mach. The Empiriocriticism of Mach and Avenarius defined the world as pure experience, going beyond Auguste Comte's original vision of a "positivist science" by eliminating the self from any role in the perception of that experience. Science no longer dealt in absolutes but in relative definitions and hypotheses; "space" and "time" were shorthand conventions to describe experience. In his philosophical study of 1908, *Materialism and Empiriocriticism*, Lenin attacked Bogdanov's attempt to combine Marxist principles with the doctrines of Mach and Avenarius. For studies of Bogdanov's views, see S. V. Utechin, "Philosophy and Society: Alexander Bogdanov," in *Revisionism: Essays on the History of Marxist Ideas*, ed. Leopold Labedz (New York: Praeger, 1962), pp. 117-25; and Dietrich Grille, *Lenins Rivale: Bogdanov und seine Philosophie* (Cologne: Wissenschaft und Politik, 1966).

56. Alexander A. Bogdanov, "Proletariat i iskusstvo," *Proletarskaia kul'tura*, no. 5 (1918), p. 32.

57. Bogdanov, "Puti proletarskogo tvorchestva," *Proletarskaia kul'tura*, nos. 15-16 (1920), pp. 50-52.

58. Bogdanov, *Iskusstvo i rabochii klass* (Moscow: Izd-vo "Proletarskaia kul'tura," 1918), p. 78.

59. Bogdanov, *Tektologiia. Vseobshchaia organizatsionnaia nauka* [Tectology. Universal Organizing Science] (Petrograd-Moscow-Berlin: Z. I. Grzhebin, 1922).

60. An excellent study of Gastev and his major role in crystallizing Soviet attitudes toward labor and work in the 1920s is Kendall E. Bailes, "Aleksei Gastev and the Soviet Controversy over Taylorism, 1918–1924," *Soviet Studies*, vol. 29 (July 1977), pp. 373-94. An important collection of Gastev's poetry and ideology is his *Poeziia rabochego udara* [Poetry of the Working Stroke], (Moscow: Izd-vo Khudozhestvennaia literatura, 1971), which is a reprint of his collected earlier poems, published in Petrograd in 1918 under the same title, together with several later key works on proletarian culture and the scientific organization of labor.

that gained wide acceptance in Soviet avant-garde art. He believed that all human society was evolving toward "collectivism," or the "collecting of man." It was possible to bring about a collective and cooperative society scientifically by consciously "organizing" a collective environment and a higher type of collective individual.

Following the February revolution of 1917 Bogdanov joined with others in founding "Proletkult," an acronym for "Proletarian Cultural and Educational Organizations," with the intention of producing a proletarian culture as the superstructural basis for the socialist revolution. After the Bolshevik seizure of power in October, the Proletkult wielded considerable influence until its loss of autonomy in 1919 following the downfall of Bogdanov. In the first two years of the revolution it promoted the creation of a proletarian culture through numerous journals and an intensive but fruitful debate on the nature of proletarian culture and art.

As the chief theoretician of Proletkult, Bogdanov enunciated its philosophy, augmenting it with aspects of sociological analysis. Regarding the Proletkult as the harbinger of a collectivist culture, Bogdanov argued that the proletariat needed a new class art based on the collectivism of labor as the embodiment of its world view and creative will. In his view, human labor had always relied on collective experience; therefore, the artistic legacy of the past should not be discarded, but should instead be scrutinized by proletarian critics to discern underlying collective principles and their organizational implications for proletarian culture.[56] The creative method in proletarian art had to be based on the collective nature of the work process in modern heavy industry; the debilitating aspects of the division of labor would be overcome by a comradely approach, predicated on conscious mutual understanding and an aspiration to work together. The resulting "monistic collectivism" would transform the whole meaning of the artist's work and give it new stimulus.[57] For Bogdanov, it was the worker who was the prime focus of proletarian culture, with the role of the artist being relegated to that of "organizing the forces in the great collective's way of life."[58] This view proved the source of the concept of art, subsequently embraced by the avant-garde, as a vital means of building, organizing, and giving material form to the new way of life (*zhiznestroenie*). Bogdanov amplified these basic ideas in 1922 with the publication of his book *Tectology*, which formulated his basic argument within the framework of what he termed a "universal organizing science."[59] Clarifying the relationship between art and labor, Bogdanov stressed that proletarian art facilitates the integral organization of the elements of the worker's life and experience in two important ways: by signifying that life experience and by providing the means to help it achieve its actual collective organization.

The concepts underlying Bogdanov's "universal organizational science" were augmented and made more vivid by Aleksei K. Gastev, a poet and industrial worker who likewise devoted himself to the idea of creating a new proletarian culture. Around 1919 Gastev emerged as the most ardent and effective exponent of the rationalization of labor and the machine as the preeminent factors in the new society.[60] His romantic vision of the machine age, epitomizing the great enthusiasm abounding in the first post-revolutionary years for employing science and technology to reform society, proved a potent source of inspiration both for exponents of production art and for the public at large by focusing on tangible implications of mechanization and labor. Gastev envisioned a new proletarian culture enlivened by rapid standardization and by an industrial urbanism realized in modern steel construction. At first this vision expressed itself in a kind of industrial poetry, capturing the country's imagination with its vivid portrayals of the new industrialism he saw arising in the Soviet state. The most popular of the so-called "worker poets," Gastev made his poems come alive with the workaday chorus of factory whistles, the hum of steel lathes, and the rhythm of steel skeletal frames. Machines were portrayed as extensions of the human body, while human beings took on mechanized attributes like "nerves of steel" and "muscles like iron nails."[61] Gastev's poetic metaphors anticipate Ginzburg's own vivid descriptions of the workers in the industrial plant in *Style and Epoch*, as, for example, in chapter six, where he writes of "endless silhouettes of the forcefully moving muscles of thousands of arms and legs."

After 1918 Gastev, in his capacity as a trade union official, took up the cause of scientific management, or Taylorism, which had been devised by American engineer Frederick W. Taylor and promoted by Russian engineers both before and after the revolution. Maintaining that the building of socialism was fundamentally synonymous with the rationalization of labor, Gastev concentrated on promulgating the scientific organization of labor (*nauchanaia organizatsiia truda*), usually abbreviated as NOT, which adapted principles of scientific management to Soviet circumstances. Gastev believed that the NOT concept, by orienting the entire social experience of the worker around his work, would form the basis for a true proletarian culture.[62] Significantly enough, NOT principles were embraced by proponents of production art, and the artist Gustav Klutsis actually worked out an elaborate chart suggesting those spheres of the new socialist society in which artists would make the most effective contributions.[63] In 1920 Gastev set up the Central Institute of Labor, which he ran for the remainder of the decade. He saw this institute as the culmination of all his earlier visions of the machine age, and the ideology he developed around it had something of the vagueness and ambiguity of poetry, an attribute which is also present in the pages of *Style and Epoch*. Gastev's institute was empowered to coordinate all Soviet research efforts at the rationalization of labor in numerous institutions throughout the country.

In 1923 Gastev extended his framework for a proletarian culture by introducing the concept of the "culture of work." Central to that concept was his belief that Soviet culture had to be infused with a new sense of inventiveness comparable to that which had inspired the work of Frederick Taylor and Henry Ford. Its most vital attributes were an earnest sense of purpose and practicality, an ability to analyze and measure in space and time, and a creative imagination capable of transforming ideas into action. The aim of such inventiveness, Gastev concluded, was the pursuit not of daydreams but of objectives that were practical, feasible, and necessary at the present time.[64] Such statements might just as well have come from Ginzburg, so fully do they accord with his ideas about the destiny of industrial and engineering structures.

The rich conceptions which filled the air in the years immediately preceding Ginzburg's writing of *Style and Epoch* were effectively synthesized in the terse credo which Alexander Vesnin presented at INKHUK in April 1922.[65] Written by a man who played a pivotal role in founding the Constructivist movement in Soviet architecture, it is possible to see this credo as a kind of prolegomenon to Ginzburg's treatise of 1924. Vesnin argued that since the tempo of modernity was rapid and dynamic, and its rhythm precise and mathematical, then modern art had to equal it and become "an active force organizing man's consciousness and provoking him into vigorous activity, acting on him like the dynamo that im-

61. One of Gastev's most popular poems, "My rastem iz zheleza" [We Grow out of Iron], celebrates the metal skeletal frame of the towering skyscraper. The original and an English translation are published in *Modern Russian Poetry*, ed. Vladimir Markov and Merrill Sparks (Indianapolis-New York: Bobbs-Merrill, 1966), pp. 698-99.

62. Gastev first advanced his concept of a proletarian culture in a 1919 article. In it, he maintained that the emerging aspects of such a culture were already evident in the mechanization and standardization of modern industry, particularly the airplane and automobile industries of America and the arms industry of the entire world. To comprehend and exploit the full implications of this new culture, it was necessary to be an engineer and a constructor or to assimilate their methods, which derived from the mechanized production process that had brought the modern proletariat into being. Gastev, "O tendentsiiakh proletarskoi kul'tury" [Concerning Tendencies in Proletarian Culture], *Proletarskaia kul'tura*, nos. 9-10 (1919), pp. 36-44.

63. Klutsis's wheel, divided into four sections titled "Daily Life," "Recreation," "Advertising," and "Agitprop" [agitational propaganda], is reproduced in Margit Rowell and Angelica Z. Rudenstine, *Art of the Avant-Garde in Russia: Selections from the George Costakis Collection* (New York: Solomon R. Guggenheim Museum, 1981), p. 273.

64. These ideas were forcefully articulated in his *Iunost'*, *idi* [Come, Youth], originally published in 1923 and reproduced in the 1971 edition of Gastev's *Poeziia rabochego udara* (see supra, n. 60), pp. 223-45; the points in question are developed on pp. 229-40.

65. Aleksandr A. Vesnin, "Kredo (1922)" [Credo (1922)], in *Mastera sovetskoi arkhitektury ob arkhitekture* [Masters of Soviet Architecture on Architecture], comp. M. G. Barkhin and Iu. S. Iaralov, vol. 2 (Moscow: Iskusstvo, 1975).

pels the machine to movement."[66] The objects created by the modern artist, he continued, were to be "pure constructions without the ballast of representation," their basic elements being material, line, surface, and texture. They were to be objects of "materialized energy, possessing dynamic properties (movement, direction, weight, speed) and determined according to their purpose." He further clarified this analogy between the conception of the art object and the machine when he wrote:

"Just as each part of the machine is materialized into a form and material corresponding to the force that functions within and is essential to the given system, and its form and material cannot be arbitrarily modified without disturbing the operation of the system as a whole, so too, in the object constructed by the artist, each element is materialized force and cannot be arbitrarily disposed of or modified without disturbing the purposive functioning of the given system, i.e., the object.

"The modern engineer has created brilliant objects: the bridge, the steam engine, the airplane, the crane.

"The modern artist must create objects that are equal to them in power, intensity, and potential in the context of their psychophysiological impact as an organizing element in man's consciousness."[67]

A Note on the Translation

This translation has been made from the first and only edition of *Stil' i epokha: problemy sovremennoi arkhitektury*, which was published in Moscow in 1924 by the State Publishing House (Gosizdat). A figurative, pictorial language enlivens all of Ginzburg's writings in the first half of the 1920s. These writings, in contrast to his publications later in the decade, manifest a rather lyrical Russian literary style; they vividly reflect the romantic and revolutionary fervor of the period. The same pictorial language likewise was typical of Ginzburg's lectures, which reportedly could entrance supporters and detractors alike.

In *Style and Epoch*, however, that language is overlaid by a way of writing little apparent in his prior or subsequently published works: namely, an infusion of Germanisms with occasional interjections of conversational speech. One also encounters a feature common to a particular style of Soviet writing in the twenties, of alternating labyrinthine sentences of great length (and poor punctuation) with short hammer blows of unqualified assertions that are italicized as key phrases. All this makes for a prose that has the resonant cadence of oratory, and the power to carry its author along by the forceful ebb and flow of his delivery.

The fact that Ginzburg's Russian is rich, animated, and at times quite convoluted has made the task of translation a very challenging one. The present effort has been aimed at achieving what in Russian is known as a "congenial translation" (*kongeal'nyi perevod*), one rendered both accurately and readably in the idiom of the translated language, but in the spirit of the original. A concerted effort has thus been made to retain as much as possible of the essential Ginzburg, since the original text is likely to remain as inaccessible as before to the majority of Western architecture students and critics simply because it is in Russian.

I am greatly indebted to my colleague Professor Caryl Emerson, who scrutinized earlier drafts of this translation sentence by sentence. Her keen knowledge of the particular genre of Soviet critical writings of the twenties, to which *Style and Epoch* bears a striking resemblance, helped clarify some of the lexical nuances of Ginzburg's mode in this work and thus to uncover, in her

The first page of chapter four of the original edition of Style and Epoch.

words, the contours of the author's particular voice. I am also in debt to Joan Ockman for her diligent editorial skills. Any errors and omissions, of course, remain the translator's.

Two terms that are central to Ginzburg's argument may fruitfully be considered at this point:

Sovremennyi. This word can be translated either as "contemporary"—that is to say, related to the present or recent times—or "modern." The second meaning, of course, goes beyond a simple description of chronology to connote something that is *new*; it is frequently used to characterize the latest styles, methods, or ideas. As the latter theme clearly is the focus of Ginzburg's book, the word has been rendered as "modern."

Konstruktivnyi. As employed throughout the text, this word expresses a very broad conceptual understanding of the process or dynamics of construction, and hence is to be distinguished from the more narrowly technical term "structural" (*strukturnyi*). There are several passages where the word "structural" would seem to have been a more natural choice; Ginzburg, however, opts for "constructive" in order to maintain a semiological consistency in his argument. "Constructive," of course, ultimately leads to both the term and the concept of Constructivism.

The original format of *Style and Epoch* is straightforward and unexceptional, the artwork seemingly put together in haste, and illustrations frequently presented to less than optimum advantage. Indeed, apart from the placement of a thematic photograph at the head of every chapter, reminiscent of Le Corbusier's *Vers une architecture*, the only significant piece of graphic design connected with the original book was the jacket designed by Alexander Vesnin. For this reason, it was decided not to produce a facsimile edition, although the essential relationship of text to illustrations has been maintained as far as possible throughout. The section of illustrations at the end presents now-scarce illustrative material, much of which has never been republished elsewhere.

The footnotes that appear in the margins are Ginzburg's, with some amplifications that were considered necessary to clarify the text. The original note style has been normalized; significant additions to the original notes and new notes are in brackets. Translator's glosses are marked by lower-case letters to distinguish them from the numbers designating the footnotes; they appear at the end of the book. All Russian titles have been transliterated, following the Library of Congress system with some minor exceptions. Ligatures used when a single Russian letter has to be rendered by two Latin letters have been eliminated. Likewise, names with well-established English translations have been rendered as such.

Anatole Senkevitch, Jr.
Ithaca, New York

66. These remarks, contained in a set of Vesnin's notes also dating from 1922, articulate more descriptively the identical theme addressed in his "Credo." They are included in the same compendium cited in n. 65, p. 15.

67. Vesnin, "Credo," p. 14. References to the psychophysiological impact on man's consciousness, which anticipate similar ones in *Style and Epoch*, reflect the position of the Left Front of the Arts, or LEF, with which Vesnin was associated. Central to the theoretical program advanced by the Left Front and its journal *LEF* (1923–1925) was the view that art offered a vital means of exerting an influence on the psyche of the proletariat, and that this influence could stimulate it to build the new life. This concept of *zhiznestroenie* was one of the major impulses behind "agitprop" art. Although the core of the LEF group consisted of the former Futurist poets led by Vladimir Mayakovsky, the term "Futurist" after the Revolution became virtually synonymous with modern art in general. As the Futurists sought to expand their role in Soviet culture, Futurism sought to encompass all avant-garde art, regardless of the medium. The journal *LEF*, conceived in this broad sense, was envisaged as an organ that would bring together all facets of Soviet avant-garde art. Through Osip Brik, then head of INKHUK and allied with its Constructivist group, *LEF* supported and promoted the work of leading Constructivist artists including architectural projects by the Vesnin brothers. Accordingly, such artists as Alexander Rodchenko, Varvara Stepanova, Liubov Popova, Alexander Lavinsky, and Alexander Vesnin gravitated toward the journal *LEF* and began, with Brik, to represent *LEF*'s position in the visual arts. It was into this circle that Ginzburg was brought by Alexander Vesnin.

М. Я. ГИНЗБУРГ

СТИЛЬ и ЭПОХА

проблемы современной архитектуры

ГОСУДАРСТВЕННОЕ ИЗДАТЕЛЬСТВО
МОСКВА

Title page of the original edition of Style
and Epoch.

Preface[1]

Architectural style and modernity? The modernity of purifying storms, when the erected buildings have scarcely numbered in the tens?

So what style can there be any talk about?

This is certainly the attitude of persons who are free from the doubts and delusions plaguing those in pursuit of new directions, of paths to new quests; it is the attitude of those who patiently await the final results with tally in hand and verdict on their lips. But their time has not yet come; their turn still lies ahead.

The pages of the present book are devoted not to what has already *been accomplished*, but only to meditations on what is *being accomplished*, meditations on the phase now proceeding from the already dead past to the emerging modernity, on the throes of the evolving *new style* dictated by the new life, a style whose aspect is still not clear but is nonetheless desired, growing and becoming stronger among those who are looking to the future with confidence.

1. The basic theses of the present work were set forth by me on May 18, 1923, in a lecture delivered at the Moscow Architectural Society [*Moskovskoe Arkhitekturnoe Obshchestvo*]; on February 8, 1924, the content of the already completed book was read by me at the Russian Academy of Artistic Sciences [*Rossiiskaia Akademiia Khudozhestvennykh Nauk*].

1.
Style.
Elements of Architectural Style.
Continuity and Independence
in the Change of Styles

A movement begins simultaneously at many points. The old is regenerated, carrying everything along with it until, finally, nothing can resist the current: the new style becomes a fact.
Why did all this have to happen?

H. Wölfflin, *Renaissance and Baroque*

Caprone triplane

For nearly two centuries architectural creativity in Europe has lived parasiti-cally off its past. At a time when the other arts somehow managed to move forward, systematically transforming their revolutionary innovators into "clas-sics," architecture persisted, with unparalleled stubbornness, in refusing to tear its sights away from the ancient world or from the epoch of the Italian Renais-sance. Academies of art were concerned with nothing more, it seems, than weeding out young people's enthusiasm for the new and leveling their aptitude for creative work without, however, teaching them to see in the creations of the past the system of legitimate development that always flows inevitably out of the vital structure of the epoch and thus derives its true meaning only in that context. Consequently, such "academic" training yielded two results: the pupil lost touch with modernity and, at the same time, remained alienated from the true spirit of the great creations of the past. This also explains why artists seek-ing to express a purely modern understanding of form in their art often deliber-ately ignore all the aesthetic accomplishments of past epochs.

However, a thoughtful examination of the art of the past and of the creative at-mosphere in which it evolved leads to different conclusions. It is precisely ex-perience, consolidated in the creative efforts of centuries, that quite clearly shows the modern artist his path—the bold quest, the daring pursuit of the new, and the joy of creative discoveries—the whole thorny path, which ends in triumph only when the movement is genuine and the aspiration vivid and washed ashore by a vital, truly mod-ern wave.

Such was the art of all the best periods of human existence, and, of course, such it must be today as well.

If we recall the harmonious environ-ment in which the Parthenon was created, how the syndicates of wool

Battleship

and silk producers competed with one another during the epoch of the Italian Renaissance for the superior realization of an aesthetic ideal, or how the women peddling vegetables and small wares responded to the new details of a cathedral under construction, then we shall clearly understand that the entire matter comes down to the fact that both the architect of the cathedral and the old woman peddling vegetables breathed the same air and were contemporaries.

True, everyone is also aware of historical examples of how the authentic prophets of new form remained misunderstood by their contemporaries, but this is merely indicative of the fact that these artists intuitively anticipated and sur-passed a modernity that, after a certain fairly significant period of time, caught up with them.

If a truly modern rhythm begins to reverberate in a modern form in unison with the rhythms of labor and the joys of the present day, then naturally it will at length also have to be heard by those whose life and toil create that rhythm. It can be said that the artist's craft and any other craft will then proceed toward a single goal, and there will inevitably come a time when, finally, all these lines will intersect, i.e., when we shall discover our *great style*, in which the acts of crea-tion and contemplation will become fused—when the architect renders his de-signs in the same style as the tailor makes his garments; when a choral song, in its rhythm, easily unites extraneous and diverse rhythms; when epic drama and street humor are embraced, for all their diversity of form, by common characteristics of one and the same language. Such are precisely the symptoms of any authentic and healthy style, in which the cause and interdependence[a] of all these phenomena will be found upon serious analysis to derive from the basic factors of the epoch.

Thus we arrive in earnest at the concept of *style*, which is so often applied in different contexts and which we shall attempt to decipher.

Indeed, at first glance, this word is full of ambiguity. We use *style* in connection with a new theatrical production, and we use *style* in regard to the fashion of a lady's hat. We often subsume in the word *style* characteristics peculiar to the most subtle nuances of art (we say, for example, "the style of the forties" or "the style of Michele Sanmicheli"), and we sometimes attribute to it the meaning of entire epochs or of a cluster of centuries (as, for example, "the Egyptian style" or "the style of the Renaissance").

In all these instances we have in mind a certain natural unity that is discernible in the phenomena under consideration.

Certain characteristics of style in art can be discerned if we compare its evolution with that of other realms of human activity, such as science, for example. Indeed, the genesis of scientific thought presupposes a continuous chain of propositions, in which each new proposition proceeds from an old one and thus outgrows the latter. Here, there is direct evidence of definite growth, of an increase in the objective value of thought. This is how chemistry outgrew alchemy and rendered it obsolete, and this is how the latest research methods have become more precise and scientific than the old ones; the individual having a command of the modern physical sciences has advanced beyond Newton or Galileo.[1] In other words, we are dealing here with the case of a single, integral, and perpetually evolving organism.

The case is somewhat different for an artistic creation, which first and foremost satisfies itself and the environment that has engendered it, as well as for a creation that actually fulfills its goals and, as such, cannot be surpassed.[2] Thus, it is extremely difficult to apply the word *progress* to art; the word is germane only in the context of the technical potentialities of art. There are certain things that are different and new in art—forms and their combinations—which sometimes cannot be anticipated; and just as an artistic creation represents something of value, so it remains unsurpassed in its particular value. Indeed, can it be said that the artists of the Renaissance surpassed the artists of Greece, or that the Temple at Karnak is inferior to the Pantheon? Of course not. It is only possible to say that just as the Temple at Karnak is the result of the particular environment that engendered it and can only be understood against the background of this environment, of its material and spiritual culture, so the perfection of the Pantheon is the result of similar factors, which are virtually independent of the merits of the Karnak temple.

It is well known that the characteristics of the flat Egyptian fresco, unfolding its narrative in horizontal bands placed one on top of another, are not symptomatic of the imperfection of Egyptian art but are simply a reflection of the characteristic Egyptian understanding of form, for which such a method proved not only the

1. Ionas Kon (Jonas Cohn), *Obshchaia estetika* [General Aesthetics], trans. Samson (Moscow: Gosizdat, 1921).
2. The distinction between science and art is discussed by Schiller. See his letters to Fichte of 3-4 August 1975 [*sic*]. (*Pis'ma* [Letters], IV, p. 222.) [Ginzburg likely was citing the Russian edition of Schiller's letters: *Polnoe sobranie pisem* (Complete Collecton of Letters), 7 vols. (St. Petersburg, 1897-).]

best, but also the only one bringing complete satisfaction. Were a modern picture to be shown to an Egyptian, it doubtless would be subjected to very harsh criticism. The Egyptian would find it to be both inexpressive and unpleasant to the eye; he would be compelled to say that the picture was a bad one. And we, conversely, in evaluating the aesthetic merits of Egyptian perspective, after having obtained a completely different conception of perspective from the artists of the Italian Renaissance, must not only comprehend all of Egyptian art as a whole, but also perform a certain feat of reincarnation; we must strive to penetrate the Egyptian's mode of perceiving the world around him. What, then, for someone investigating the arts, should be the interrelationship between an Egyptian and a Renaissance fresco? Naturally, the commonly accepted meaning of the word *progress* is not applicable here, as we certainly could not argue objectively that the Egyptian fresco is "worse" than that of the Renaissance, or that the Renaissance system of perspective obliterates the Egyptian system of frescoes and divests it of its appeal. On the contrary, we know that along with the one developed in the Renaissance there exists a different kind of perspective system, e.g., that of the Japanese, which has been charting its own course; that we are capable even today of deriving pleasure from Egyptian mural painting; and finally, that modern artists sometimes intentionally distort the system of Italian perspective in their own work. At the same time, a person making use of the achievements in electricity cannot, under any circumstances, be forced to revert to steam power, which must in any case be recognized objectively as having been superseded and thus incapable of instilling in us either a sense of admiration or a desire to imitate it. It is quite apparent that we are dealing here with different kinds of phenomena.

This difference between two kinds of human activity—the artistic and the scientific—does not, however, prevent us from taking this opportunity to affirm the fact that the art of the Italian Renaissance contributed its share to the universal method of creative work and enriched it with a new system of perspective that was unknown prior to that time.

Thus, we are ultimately dealing here with *a certain growth, expansion, and enrichment of art*, which is quite real and objectively discernible, but which does not abolish in the process the previously existing method of creative work. Accordingly, it is possible to speak in a certain sense of the evolution of art, of the progress of art, quite apart from its technical aspect.

Only this progress or evolution can culminate in the capacity to evolve new values and new creative systems, thereby enriching mankind as a whole.

However, this enrichment, this emergence of the new in art cannot be called forth by chance, by a fortuitous invention of new forms and new creative methods.

We have already said that the Egyptian fresco, like the fifteenth-century Italian painting, can be understood and hence receive the benefit of objective evaluation only after all the art contemporary with it has been comprehended as a whole. Frequently, however, even this is not enough. It is necessary to become acquainted with all the realms of human activity that were contemporary with the given painting, with the social and economic structure of the epoch and its climatic and national characteristics, in order fully to comprehend it. A person appears to be one way and not another not because of the "fortuitousness" of his birth, but as a result of the highly complex influences he has experienced, the so-

40

cial environment surrounding him, and the effects of natural and economic conditions. Only the sum total of all these factors can engender a particular spiritual disposition in a person and beget in him a particular world outlook and system of artistic thought that guides human genius in one direction or another.

However great the collective or individual genius of the creator, however original and resilient the creative process, *there is a causal interdependence between practical, real-life factors and a man's system of artistic thought, and, in turn, between the latter and the formal creative work of an artist;* and it is precisely the existence of this interdependence that explains both the character of the evolution of art that we have spoken about and the need for a transformation that fosters the objective historical evaluation of a work of art. However, this interdependence must not be understood in too elementary a manner. The same basic causes are sometimes capable of eliciting different results: misfortune can at times sap our strength and at other times build it up many times over, depending upon the particular character traits of the individual. In precisely the same manner, we can, depending upon the nature of the genius peculiar to either an individual or a people, detect one result in some instances and, conversely, the opposite result in others. In both instances, however, it is not possible to dismiss the presence of this causal interdependence which provides the only background against which a work of art can be evaluated, not on the basis of a personal judgment of taste, in terms of "liking" it or "not liking" it, but as an objective historical phenomenon. Formal comparisons can only be made among works of art belonging to a single epoch or a single style; only within these limits is it possible to establish formal attributes for works of art. The better ones among them, the ones responding most expressively to the system of artistic thought that engendered them, are usually those which have acquired a better formal language. It is not possible, from a qualitative standpoint, to compare an Egyptian fresco and an Italian painting. Doing so would only produce one result: it would point to two distinct systems of artistic creation, each one having its own sources in a different environment.

This is why it is impossible for a modern artist to create an Egyptian fresco; this is why eclecticism, however brilliant its representatives, is genetically barren in most instances. It does not create anything "new," does not enrich art and, consequently, in the *evolutionary course of art*, yields not a plus but a minus, not an expansion but a compromising combination of often incompatible aspects.

An examination of the most varied products of human activity in any epoch, particularly any forms of artistic endeavor, reveals that despite the diversity brought about by organic and individual causes, they all have something in common, some indication that, in its collective social origins,[b] gives rise to the concept of style. The same social and cultural conditions, methods and means of production, and climate, the same outlook and psychology all leave a common mark on the most diverse formations. Consequently, it is not surprising that the archaeologist who, a thousand years later, uncovers a pitcher or a statue or a fragment of clothing will be able, on the basis of such common characteristics, to attribute these objects to one epoch or another. Wölfflin, in his examination of the Renaissance and Baroque, has shown the range of human activity in which it is possible to trace the characteristics of style: he says that the manner of standing or walking, of draping a coat in one way or another, of wearing a narrow or wide shoe, of each sundry detail—all these can serve as indications of a style. Thus,

41

3. Osval'd Shpengler (Oswald Spengler), *Zakat Evropy* [The Decline of the West], vol. 1; Russian trans. [by L. D. Frenkel, (Moscow-Petrograd: Mospoligraf)], 1923.
4. N[ikolai] Ia. Danilevskii, *Rossiia i Evropa*. [*Vzgliad na kul'turnyia i politicheskiia otnosheniia sliavanskogo mira k germanskomu*. Russia and Europe. A View of the Cultural and Political Relations between the Slavic and German Worlds] (3d ed. [St. Petersburg: "Obshchestvennaia pol'za"], 1888).

the word *style* signifies certain kinds of natural phenomena that impose definite traits on all manifestations of human activity, large and small, quite irrespective of whether or not their contemporaries might have aspired to or even have been at all aware of them. Nevertheless, the laws eliminating "chance" from the creation of any man-made product assume their own concrete expressiveness for each facet of creative activity. Thus, a musical work is organized in one way, and a literary work in another. Yet in these rather different laws, engendered by differences in the formal method and language of each art form, can be discerned certain common, unified premises, something crystallizing the whole and binding it together—in other words, a *unity of style* in the broad sense of the word.

Thus, the determination of the style of an artistic phenomenon can be regarded as being definitive when it includes not only an illumination of the organizational laws of that phenomenon, but also the establishment of a definite link between these laws and the given historical epoch, and a verification of them through a comparison with other forms of creative work and human activity contemporaneous with that epoch. It certainly is not too difficult to verify this relationship for any of the historical styles. The indivisible connection between the monuments of the Acropolis, the statues of Phidias or Polykleitos, the tragedies of Aeschylus and Euripides, the economy and culture of Greece, its political and social order, its clothing and utensils and sky and terrain, is just as indestructible, in our view, as that between analogous phenomena of any other style.

Such a method of analyzing artistic phenomena, because of its relative objectivity, supplies the investigator with powerful tools for dealing with more controversial questions as well.

Thus, proceeding from such a point of view to developments in our own artistic life during the preceding decades, it is possible to recognize, without any particular difficulty, that such tendencies as the "Moderne"[c] and the "Decadence,"[d] as well as all our "neo-classicisms" and "neo-Renaissances," cannot in any way stand the test of modernity. Having originated in the minds of a few highly cultivated and refined architects and, as a result of their considerable talent, often yielding rather accomplished images in their own right, this superficial aesthetic crust, like all other possible eclectic manifestations, represents an idle invention that appealed for a time to the taste of a narrow circle of connoisseurs but did not reflect anything other than the decadence and impotence of an obsolescent world.

In this manner, we discern a certain self-sufficiency [e] of style, the uniqueness of the laws governing it, and the relative isolation of its formal manifestations from the products of other styles. We discard the purely individualistic evaluation of a work of art and consider the ideal of the beautiful, that eternally changeable and transitory ideal, as *something that perfectly fulfills the requirements and concepts of a given place and epoch.*

Questions naturally arise: What is the relationship between the individual manifestations of art in the different epochs? And are Spengler[3] and Danilevsky[4] not correct in their theories, isolated and separated though they are from one another by a gap in cultures?

Although we have established the exclusivity of the laws of any style, we are naturally far from entertaining the notion of renouncing the principle of interdependence and influence in the changes and developments of these styles. On the contrary, the precise limits between one style and another are blurred in actual reality. It is not possible to fix the moment when one style ends and another begins; style, once born, lives out its youth, maturity, and old age; but old age is still not fully spent, atrophy not yet complete, when another new style arises to assume a similar course. Hence, in reality, not only is there a link between consecutive styles, but it is even difficult to establish a precise boundary between them, as is the case in the evolution of all forms of life, without exception. When we speak of the self-sufficient significance of style, we naturally have in mind a synthetic conception of it, the quintessence of its true nature, which is reflected primarily in the peak phase of its flowering and in the best works of that phase. Thus, in speaking of the Greek style, we have in mind the fifth century B.C., the century of Phidias, Ictinos, Callicrates, and their age, rather than the withering Hellenistic art, which already contained many characteristics anticipating the emergence of the Roman style. In any event, the wheels of the two consecutive styles become coupled, and the circumstances of this coupling are rather interesting to follow.

We shall limit ourselves, in the present instance, to considering this question in the context of architecture, which is the subject of greatest interest to us.

To do so, however, it is necessary at the outset to elucidate those concepts that enter into the formal definition of an architectural style. We are already quite well aware of what distinguishes a painterly[f] style: we speak of drawing, color, composition, and all these aspects are naturally subjected to the analysis of the investigator. It likewise is not difficult to convince ourselves of the fact that the first of these, drawing and color, are the basic elements whose organization on a surface constitutes the art of composing a painterly work. So, too, in architecture it is essential to make note of a whole number of concepts without whose elucidation the formal analysis of its products is inconceivable.

The need to create shelter from the rain and cold induced man to build a dwelling. And this need has determined to the present day the very character of architecture, which hovers on the edge between vitally useful creative work and a "disinterested" art. This aspect was first reflected in the need *to isolate, to enclose a certain portion of space with some substantive material forms.* To isolate space, to enclose it within certain specific boundaries, constitutes the first of the problems confronting the architect. The organization of isolated space, of the crystalline form that envelops what is essentially amorphous space, is the characteristic that distinguishes architecture from the other arts. That which establishes the particular character of *spatial experiences,* so to speak, the sensations derived from the interiors of architectural works, from being inside buildings, from their spatial boundaries, and from the system illuminating this space—all this constitutes the primary indication, the primary distinguishing characteristic of architecture, which does not recur in the perceptions of any other art.

But the isolation of space, the method of its organization, is accomplished by means of utilizing material form: wood, stone, brick. In isolating the spatial prism, the architect clothes it in material form. Thus, we unavoidably perceive this prism not only from within, in spatial terms, but also from without, in purely volumetric terms, analogously to the way we perceive sculpture. Here, too, however, there exists a distinction of vital importance between architecture and the other arts. The material forms used to solve the architect's basic spatial problems are not altogether arbitrary in their composition. It is essential that the architect comprehend the laws of statics and mechanics in order to accomplish his objectives empirically, whether in an intuitive or strictly scientific manner. Doing so represents that fundamental constructive sensibility which must, without fail, be basic to the architect and *which establishes a definite method* in his work. The solution of the spatial problem will inevitably involve this particular organizational method as well, entailing a solution with the minimal expenditure of energy.

Thus, what essentially distinguishes the architect from the sculptor is not only the *organization of space, but also the construction of its isolating environment.* Out of this evolves the basic organizational method of the architect, for whom the world of form represents not a series of unlimited and endless possibilities, but merely a skillful attempt to strike a balance between what is desirable and what is possible to implement; it is quite natural that, in the final analysis, what is possible influences the development of the very character of what is desirable. Accordingly, the architect never builds even "castles in the air" that cannot be developed within the framework of this organizational method; even architectural fantasy itself, seemingly devoid of constructive considerations, satisfies the laws of statics and mechanics, and this already points to a characteristic that is unquestionably fundamental and most essential to understanding the art of architecture. This also explains the relatively limited range of forms in architecture as compared to painting, as well as the basic approach to conceiving of architectural forms as functions of that which supports and that which is supported, of that which is holding up and that which is lying prone, of that which is in tension and that which is at rest, of the vertical and the horizontal extension of forms, and of any other aspects operating as functions of these basic tendencies. *This organizational method also conditions those rhythmic aspects by which architecture is distinguished. Finally, it already determines, to some extent, the character of each individual formal molecule, which is always distinct from the elements of sculpture or painting.*

Thus, the system of architectural style is made up of a series of aspects, spatial and volumetric, which represent the solution of one and the same problem both from within and from without, and are materialized by formal elements; these elements are organized according to various sets of compositional characteristics, giving rise to the *dynamic problem of rhythm.*

Only an understanding of architectural style in all these complex aspects can explain not only a given style, but also the relationship of one individual stylistic phenomenon to another. Thus, analyzing the change from the Greek to the Roman style, from the Romanesque to the Gothic, and so forth, we often discern contradictory aspects. For example, the Roman style is, on the one hand, viewed by investigators as an evolution of the pure forms of the Hellenic legacy; yet on the other hand, it is impossible not to call attention to the fact that the compositional methods and the organization of space in Roman buildings are the virtual antithesis of those established by the Greeks.

In precisely the same way, the art of the early Renaissance in Italy (the Quattrocento) was still filled with isolated aspects of the moribund Gothic style, while the methods of Renaissance composition already seemed so new and so unexpected as compared to the Gothic, their spatial experiences so altogether different, that they elicited in a contemporary—the architect Filarete—the famous statement concerning the Gothic: "cursed be the one who invented this nonsense. I think that only barbaric people could have brought it with them to Italy."[5]

From this vantage point there looms, in addition to the evaluation of a work of art or an entire style *historically*, i.e., with respect to the environment that created it, yet another method of objective evaluation—the *genetic one*, i.e., the method determining the value of a phenomenon from the standpoint of its relationship to the further growth of a style, to the evolution of a general process. And in view of the fact that an artistic style, like any vital phenomenon, is not regenerated all at once or in all its manifestations, but relies more or less partially on the past, it is possible to distinguish which styles are more or less valuable in a genetic sense, insofar as they possess the qualities more or less suitable for regeneration, the potential for creating something new. Clearly this evaluation is not always made with respect to the quality of the formal elements in a work of art. Frequently, that which is formally weak—i.e., an imperfect or incomplete work—may be of greater value genetically—i.e., by virtue of its potential for creating something new—than a monument that may be impeccable, but which nonetheless employs highly obsolete material from the past and is incapable of further creative development.

What, then, do we have here? Is it continuity or new and utterly independent principles that underlie the change from one style to another?

It is both, of course. At a time when some of the constituent elements generating style still maintain continuity, other elements, which are more sensitive and which more rapidly reflect the changes in human life and psychology, already are taking form according to principles that are quite different, often contrary, and often entirely new in the history of the evolution of styles; and only after a certain length of time, when the incisiveness of the new compositional method has reached the fullness of its development, is it then passed on to the remaining elements of style as well, to an individual form, subjecting it to the same laws of development and even modifying it according to the new aesthetic of style. Conversely, it is frequently the case that various laws of the new style are reflected, first and foremost, in entirely different formal elements, initially maintaining a continuity with past compositional methods and only gradually becoming modified in the ensuing phase. Yet irrespective of which of these routes art might follow, the appearance of a new and consummate style is possible only as a result of both these principles—*continuity* and *independence*. The complex phenomenon of architectural style cannot change at once and in all respects. The *law of continuity* economizes the creative inventiveness and resourcefulness of the artist, consolidating his experience and skill, while the *law of independence* constitutes that motive force which gives creativity its healthy, youthful juices and saturates it with that poignant aspect of modernity without which art simply ceases to be art. The flowering of a style, condensed in a brief period of time, will usually reflect these *new and independent laws of creative work*, while the archaic and decadent aspects of the epoch, whether in isolated formal elements or compositional methods, will be linked to both preceding and ensuing stylistic periods. That is how this apparent contradiction is reconciled and finds its explanation not only in the emergence of a new style, but in any historical epoch as well.

Were it not for a certain continuity, the evolution of each culture would remain forever infantile, perhaps never once reaching the summit of that flowering

5. [Although Ginzburg does not cite his source for this statement by Filarete, it probably was Gustav J. von Allesch, *Die Renaissance in Italien* (Weimar: G. Kiepenhauer, 1912), a work to which Ginzburg refers in chapter 2. Von Allesch's book includes an excerpt from Filarete's treatise, entitled "Antonio Filarete an Francesco Sforza in Mailand" (pp. 209-11), which ends with this particular statement about Gothic, or more precisely, "modern" architecture.]

6. Letter of Leone Battista Alberti to Matteo de Bastia (de' Pasti) in Rimini (Rome, 18 November 1454). In a letter to Brunelleschi (1436), Alberti states, "I believe that our merit should be all the greater if, without teachers and without any models, we could discover arts and sciences hitherto unheard of and unseen." [Although Ginzburg does not cite the source for these two quotations, again it is probably von Allesch's *Die Renaissance in Italien*, which includes both letters: "Leon Battisti Alberti an Filippo Brunellesco (Florence, 1436)," pp. 98-100; and "Leon Battista Alberti an Matteo de Bastia zu Rimini (Rome, 18 November 1454?)," pp. 103-5.

7. Fransua Benua (François Benoit), *Franzuzkoe iskusstvo vremen revoliutsii* [French Art from the Period of the Revolution]. Trans. by S. Platonova being prepared for publication. [Perusal of *Knizgnaia letopis'* (Book Annals) for the period of 1924-1934 failed to turn up the publication of the above Russian translation; nor have any other references to it turned up in Soviet scholarly or bibliographical literature of the period. The original French edition of Benoit's book is entitled *L'Art Français sous la Révolution et l'Empire* (Paris: Librairie G. Baranger, 1897); mention of the transformation of St. Hilaire cited by Ginzburg occurs in fn. 2, p. 11.]

which is attained only as a result of the consolidation of the artistic experience of preceding cultures.

Yet at the same time, were it not for this independence, cultures would fall into a state of perpetual old age and helpless atrophy lasting forever, since it is impossible to chew perpetually on the same old food. What is needed, at all costs, is the daring blood of barbarians who do not know what they are creating, or people who have a relentless penchant for creative work and an awareness of the legitimacy of their emerging and independent "self," so that art can become renewed once again and enter anew into its period of flowering. This makes it possible to comprehend psychologically not only the destructive barbarians, whose blood pulses with the assured legitimacy of their potential strength, even in relation to refined but decrepit cultures, but also the entire gamut of "vandalisms" that are so often encountered in the history of the most highly civilized epochs, when the new destroys the old, even the beautiful and the sublime, merely on the strength of the legitimacy granted to youthful daring.

Let us recall what was said by Alberti, the representative of a culture which possessed so many elements of continuity, but which in its essence serves as an example of the establishment of a new style: "I have more faith in those who built the Thermae and the Pantheon and all the other edifices . . . and in reason a great deal more than in any person."[6]

The same growing confidence in the correctness of his own creative stance often prompted Bramante, in realizing his grandiose projects, to tear down entire blocks, and earned him the nickname "Ruinante" among his detractors. But the same nickname could just as well have been applied to any of the leading architects of the Cinquecento or Seicento. Palladio, after the fire of 1577 at the Doge's Palace in Venice, repeatedly counseled the Senate to rebuild the Gothic palace in the spirit of its own particular Renaissance world outlook—in Roman forms. In 1661 Bernini, faced with the task of building the colonnade in front of St. Peter's basilica, demolished Raphael's Palazzo dell'Aquila without any particular doubts or hesitation. Many more such instances occurred in France, of course, during the period of the Revolution. In 1797, for example, the old church of St. Hilaire in Orleans was transformed into a modern market.[7]

Even if we were to disregard this extreme manifestation of a staunch faith in the legitimacy of the creative ideas of modernity, however, any glance we might cast on the past would convince us of the existence in the highest periods of human culture of a remarkably well-defined sense of the legitimacy of an independent, modern understanding of form. Only decadent epochs are distinguished solely by a desire to subordinate modern form to the stylistic complex of past centuries; the very idea of subjecting the treatment of new sections of a city not to the latter's own organism, which lies beyond the realm of any formal specificities of style, but to the style of old, existing sections, even those which are the most formally developed—an idea that became firmly rooted in the minds of our best architects in the preceding decade and often caused them to subject their treatment of entire blocks and sections of the city to the formal aspects of some group of stylistic monuments from the past—is an excellent indication of modernity's creative impotence. In the best periods, architects have mastered previously created stylistic forms on the strength of the power and acuity of their modern genius, while still correctly anticipating the organic development of the city as a whole.

46

What is more, the artist who is filled to the core with his own creative ideas and with the reality that surrounds him cannot work in any other way. He works only on things that are on his mind, he can create only modern forms, and least of all does he become preoccupied with what others, even his most brilliant predecessors, would have done in his place.

In this sense, the Greek temple, imbued with a certain tradition, has for a number of centuries provided a most interesting case in point. Constructed over an extended period of time, the temple sometimes yields a vivid chronology of that construction through its columns.

It is perfectly clear that the Greek architect was concerned neither with any sense of continuity nor with subjecting his design to any particular sense of harmony; he was filled with a rapt and persistent desire to realize at each point in time what for him was a modern form. Inasmuch as the creative outlook of Hellas on the whole remained unified, continuity and harmony emerged in their own right.

In precisely the same way, those cathedrals begun in the epoch of the Romanesque style and completed a century or two later unavoidably assumed the character of the contemporary Gothic style, just as Renaissance architects, without a moment's hesitation, completed the cathedrals begun in the epoch and forms of the Gothic style in the purest forms of the Renaissance, which were utterly alien to these cathedrals. Naturally, these architects could not have behaved in any other way, because true creativity cannot be anything but sincere and, as a result, modern. All other considerations seem insignificant in comparison to this persistently felt desire to manifest one's own creative character. A flower grows in the field because it cannot help but grow; thus, it cannot contemplate whether or not it is appropriate to the field that existed before it. On the contrary, by its very appearance, the flower transforms the general image of the field.

An interesting phenomenon from this point of view is the philosophy of early Italian Futurism, which ran to the other extreme. Reared on and surrounded by a countless array of perfect monuments from the past, the Italian artists believed that it was these very monuments that by their perfection weighed too heavily on the artist's psyche and thus did not allow him to create a modern art; hence, the tactical decision to do away with all of this heritage. One must sack all the museums and destroy all the monuments in order to be able to create anything new! Certainly this desperate gesture is psychologically understandable because it demonstrates the artists' conscious craving for genuine creativity; but alas, it also portrays equally well the creative impotence of this art, as well as the eclectic thrusts of the passéists.[g]

Neither a concern for continuity nor the destruction of the art of the past can help in any way. These are but symptoms indicating that we have fully arrived at a new era. Only a spark of creative energy born of modernity and producing artists capable of working *not in whatever style they like but only in the innate language of modernity, reflecting in the methods of their art the true essence of the present day, its rhythm, its everyday labor and concerns, and its lofty ideals—* only such a spark can generate a new flowering, a new phase in the evolution of forms, a new and genuinely modern style. And perhaps the time is already close at hand when we shall enter into this blessed realm.

2.
The Greco-Italic "Classical" System of Thought and Its Modern Legacy

Events acquire clarity through historical perspective. Everything minor and transitory disappears; what remains in view is that which has withstood the test of time and has subsequently become more or less constant in its objective value. Years, decades, and even entire centuries play an insignificant role in this process; we see the evolution of styles in terms of their genetic development, and chronological dates serve only as points of orientation. A few outstanding monuments may sometimes provide us with such frames of reference, but we must establish the remaining evolution of this genesis through interpretation.

This is due partially, of course, to the inadequacy of our knowledge of the past. Just as the archaeological excavations undertaken in the nineteenth century enriched us by yielding a whole world of treasures from the Cretan-Minoan culture and the Egyptian world, so too a whole series of further discoveries still awaits us. As a result of such discoveries, the evolution of styles will doubtless be enriched by new periods, new phases, and perhaps even entirely new flowerings of styles.

Still, owing perhaps to the very relativity of our information about the past, a clear, synthetic pattern of the development of styles emerges. New discoveries may clarify and complicate this pattern, but they do not obscure it. That which does not possess any objective value rarely attracts our attention, even though it may conceivably have dominated the thinking of contemporaries for some brief period of time. Or conversely, something that may never have been considered by contemporaries may well enter our field of vision as a result of an impartial reckoning, of our unbiased verification of its manifestations in a whole number of other phenomena. Only by virtue of such a process is the construction of a coherent evolution of the arts even thinkable, one where

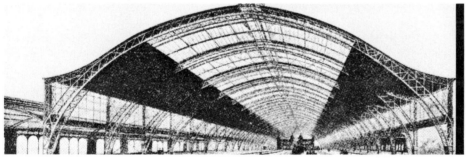

Station platform in Cologne-on-the-Rhine

each link would be perceived according to its objective signification[a] rather than its chronological period. There surely must have been a multitude of periods, decades, and even centuries in our past when the creative realm was impoverished, and everything created at the time utterly and banefully transitory. Such periods simply fall out of the genetic line we have constructed without disrupting it in any way, as this imaginary line is developed by using the coordinates of only the most successful periods. Consequently, this line traces only the most brilliant accomplishments rather than the entire gamut of developments in the creative life of a nation.

This is why historical fluctuations in style are so constant and orderly, and why the laws of continuity and independence governing them, about which we spoke in the preceding chapter, are so distinct.

Naturally, the situation is rather different in actual reality. In periods of impoverished creative capacity, it frequently seemed to people that a pitch-black night had descended over the earth: the twilight of a fading day seemed to augur the end of the world. Ferrero wrote, "In the midst of a change in civilization, people are always fearful of complete annihilation."[1]

That which we now recognize to have constituted a new link in the continuing evolution of creative life seemed to contemporaries to be an utterly impenetrable boundary, for time looms as a formidable factor when viewed in relation to historically insignificant vantage points, to prosaic daily occurrences, and to the length of a human life. At the same time, a change in styles, even if it has proven to be the destiny of those contemporaries who nurtured it, has for that very reason always been perceived as something quite revolutionary, dividing people into two irreconcilable camps—those standing on the sidelines in the shadow of bygone cultures, and those forging new links.

We, too, are experiencing such a time. If we turn to architecture, which is what interests us here, we shall see that the signs pointing to the end of one epoch and the beginning of another have for some time now been quite clearly in evidence.

For several centuries now, we have been nourishing ourselves on the juices of that antique or so-called classical system which became the springboard for the development of European architecture. If we speak of something that is either European or non-European, historical or non-historical, beautiful or ugly, we do so wholly within the framework of this "classical" system of thought, which not only became a perfected philosophical system of architecture, but also devised a brilliant alphabet for this system, from alpha to omega. In order to determine precisely which aspects of our past are of genetic value to us and which ones have been irretrievably lost, we shall now endeavor to dwell at some length on an analysis of the genesis and development of this "classical" system.

In order to elucidate the general character of classical thought, whose main theater of activity was the Greco-Italic world, it is necessary to indicate the two principal cultures that, in one form or another, participated continuously in its development. The first encompassed the *legacy of the antique Hellenic world*, a world perpetually steeped in the juices of ancient and absolute genius. The second comprised the youthful and virulent blood of the *barbaric northerners*.

The first culture came from the peninsula, islands, and archipelagoes of Greece and Asia Minor, as well as from the breeding ground of Hellenism—Greater Greece (*Magna Graecia*)—which had spilled over into Italy itself; in short, it spread its influence from the south.[2]

The second culture, a far more meager and insignificant one, had, from the earliest known times of Liguria, flowed continuously from the Alps and the various northern countries. Although it destroyed and vandalized the perfected Hellenic culture, this culture nonetheless proved significant by virtue of serving to rejuvenate weak blood. The Aryans—the Umbrians and Sabelians from the north and the Etruscans from the east—had participated long before the birth of Christ in forming the great Italic people. Thereafter, the Gauls, Germans, Goths, Huns, Franks, and Langobards continuously infiltrated Italic blood.

Whole volumes have been written on Hellenic culture and art. The perfection of the Greek artistic genius has become a commonplace. Here we shall merely attempt to highlight those of its aspects that we regard to be significant in the context of their having exerted an influence on so-called classical art.

One of the most basic aspects of all Greek art is *abstractness*. The detachment from any concrete situation, the objectivization of the environment as a whole, and the subordination of all manifestations of beauty to orderly and abstract

1. [Guglielmo] Ferrero, *Velichie i padenie Rima*. [The Greatness and Decline of Rome. As the title is rendered in Russian in the text, it is likely that Ginzburg is referring to the Russian translation by A. Zakharov (Moscow: M. & S. Sabashnikov, 1915); the original Italian ed. of Ferrero's work is *Grandezza e decadenza di Roma*, 5 vols. (Milan: Fratelli Treves, 1902-1907).]
2. The Achaean cities in Italy include Sybaris, Crotona, Metapontum, Siris, and others; the Doric colony of Tarentum; the colonies of Chalcis near Vesuvius; and the like.

51

3. [Gustav J. von Allesch, *Die Renaissance in Italien*, pp. 15-16.]

principles are distinguishing attributes of all Hellenic art.

We never experience isolated impressions, uncoordinated perceptions, or casual emotions when examining the art of the Greeks. We are always confronted with a clear regulating principle, a kind of infinitely sensible organizing scheme to which all the parts are subordinated. To perceive a Greek work of art is always to perceive such a perfected scheme, to which all details and elements of chance are subordinated.

The Greek artist was the first to understand that the world around him was not chaos, not an endless accumulation, but a harmonious and clearly organized system. He sought to isolate it within the amorphous confines of cosmic space in a way that would endow spatial experience with a perceptual clarity and precision.

The Greek genius created a grammar of art. It dissected images, classified them, and indicated their generalizing and abstracting tendencies.

It found, in a whole series of individual organisms, basic traits and attributes that were evident in each and essential to them all. It thus allowed for the coordination of similar attributes, and their combination came to represent a formula for this type of organism. It focused all its attention, in the course of many centuries of evolution, on the infinite perfection of this formula, all of whose parts and interrelationships were canonized.

Let us glance at the immortal specimens of Greek sculpture. Are we able to tell by looking at them that people can be either thin or fat, tall or short, sad or happy? Of course not, for the body sculpted by the Greeks is an abstraction of everyday experience, a formula for the human body, an infinitely perfected objectivization of a selective perception. In man, as in any other object of art, the Greeks sought out only those features that served to confirm the harmonious formula they had established.

This characteristic of the Greek genius had an even greater effect on architecture, as the very essence of this art called for the supreme objectivization of concepts.

I cite a description of the Greek temple that Allesch has rendered in his book *The Renaissance in Italy:*
"If we glance at the system, we can see that its fundamental principle encompasses a very clear articulation of the whole, a differentiation of its essential parts and a corresponding accentuation of all its joints, and a clear indication of each separate function. The way the building itself is put together and its distinguishing characteristics thus become readily apparent. We are dealing here with the conception of a systematic frame of mind that sharply differentiates attributes and does not allow them to be lumped together. . . . The Greek temple is lucid as a concept; it is also immutable and, if you will, timeless as a concept. It is so thoroughly articulated and its parts are so perfectly calculated that it is impossible to move, enlarge, or reduce a single component part without destroying the whole."[3]

Thus, we see that in architecture as well, the Greeks sought the universally compelling aspect,[b] the perfected scheme, the clearly articulated canon. These achievements in Hellenic architecture are all the more significant in view of the fact that the creative work involved here had nothing to do with any imitative impulses.

Thus, the infinite significance of the Hellenic genius in architecture stems precisely from its sense of abstraction, its articulate crystallization of space, and its *development of a formula, a system*, for the architectural monument, while the immortality of this creative effort derives from the *perfection* attained by that formula. This perfection, however, was attained over an extended period of exploration and unwavering effort; it is not surprising, therefore, that these achievements should have been *raised to the level of a system*, that all the parts of the whole should have been determined with precision on the basis of numerical ratios, and that these ratios should, in turn, have been determined by a definite order.

Thus evolved the concept of the Greek temple, which constitutes the very essence of Hellenic architecture.

The temple, portico, propylaeum, and treasury were for the Hellene all part of a whole,[c] chance happenings subordinated to a more universal scheme. The clearly defined spatial system and the specific combination of column, capital, architrave, frieze, cornice, and pediment were deemed both immutable and binding in order that nothing might be concealed from view.

If the Greek architect wished to surpass his predecessors with his own art, he naturally could not do away with such a great scheme, where everything was functionally related. Hence, he confined himself to repeating the same conception, but doubling or tripling its size and almost mechanically repeating the minutest details by enlarging them two or three times as well. Even such aspects of the subjective and particular as steps or a door, for example, were abstracted to the point of bearing no real relationship to their actual size. In this manner, the Greek temple, so well integrated into its surrounding landscape, was nonetheless deprived of an architectural sense of scale, which is obtained by taking the sizes of the various parts of a monument realistically into account.

To be sure, it is essential to note that certain variations or peculiarities arose in the conception of the Greek temple as a result of the heterogeneity of the Hellenic people and of geographic, social, and other circumstances. The Ionic order was created on the shores and islands of Asia Minor and in eastern Greece; the Doric order, in western Greece and in Sicily and the adjoining islands; in mainland Greece, the one could be found as readily as the other.[4]

Yet when we scrutinize the differences between these two orders—the Ionic and the Doric—we realize that, in essence, the scheme or formula as such has not been violated. The Greek architect barely modified the system for differentiating and correlating different parts; and despite the differences in detail from one temple to another, we are infinitely awed in all of them by the same schematized, clearly delimited space.

There are other differences as well, differences not in the orders but in the proportions relating the individual parts that evolved during the various periods of Hellenic culture, differences that evoke various sensations within us, that detail style in terms of its antiquity, its flowering, and its decline. Yet even these distinctions are powerless to destroy or modify the basic scheme.

4. The Corinthian order, which likewise evolved in Greece, possessed a purely episodic significance for Hellenic architecture and was applied principally to small monuments of a decorative nature.

The columns might be more massive, the intercolumniation greater, and the forms richer, but still the formula integrating all these details remains unchanged. It absorbs all individual, chance developments and makes this an all-embracing, universally compelling, and truly great art. The leitmotif that runs through all these differences and peculiarities is the truly exceptional sense of *inner fulfillment and equilibrium* that permeates this art, which does not aspire to the impossible, is self-contained, and reflects with utmost clarity the social order, the democratic character, and the cultural development of the Greek republics.

This serves to explain the vitality of Hellenic art, a tribute to those spellbinding qualities acknowledged by every people and every nation.

By embodying an infinitely perfect, abstract, universally compelling, timeless, extranational, and almost inhumanly harmonious formula, Hellenic art deprived itself of a certain degree of flexibility; the Greek temple could be repeated precisely, but it could never be modified or stylized. This is why the Italian Renaissance, given its creative sensibilities and tact, never once reproduced the formula for the Greek temple in its art, despite the powerful infiltration of Hellenic influence and the close proximity of the magnificent temples at Paestum.

The more primitive the level of human culture, the more prevalent the ascendancy of the characteristics of race, nature, and climate, which marshal the national aspects of creative temperament and only slowly and gradually yield their preeminence to the influence of the social and economic characteristics of a life grown increasingly complex.

In comparison with the abstractness, clarity, and purity of the Greek architectural schemes, the northern influence exerted by the transalpine peoples supplied Italy with quite the opposite characteristics. Instead of abstract concepts, one always encounters in the art of these peoples a highly idiosyncratic form teeming with subjective aspects. If the Greek sought out generalized characteristics, the northerner, brought up in a tense struggle with the ever-subjective and concrete peculiarities of a severe climate, on the contrary sought out random combinations characteristic of a particular moment. The northerner was always an impressionist, for he snatched an isolated moment from the world around him or from his own experience. He aspired wholeheartedly to convey the emotions linked, in his view, to a given subjective conception. While the Hellene aspired to discover a *formula, a scheme, virtually the idea of form itself,* the northern artist wished to convey a *spiritual representation* of some image arousing his own real emotion. This is why Greek art is always rather cold and rational, with the harmony of the scheme emerging as its ideal; northern art, on the other hand, is always expressive and emotional, warmed by the glow of feeling, and generating *pathos* as its highest achievement.

Instead of the clear and pristine formula devised by the Greeks, we see its violation here: confused and strained features, a disregard of universal laws, and a yearning for the poignancy and expressiveness of form at all cost.

If in the Greek's representation the human body constitutes something of a perfected mechanism whose laws and functions are evident, what the northern artist sees in man is merely a kind of emotional impulse, a kind of yearning, to whose

54

poignancy everything else is subordinated.

5. [Von Allesch, ibid.]

What kind of architecture, then, can be expected to evolve at the hands of the northerners? It is above all always indigenous; it always expresses a particular creative moment, a particular creative atmosphere, which it then unfailingly seeks to stress at the expense of any general or abstract characteristics.

Although the monuments of the Athenian Acropolis are indeed firmly linked to the contours of their surrounding landscape, there is, however, nothing extraordinary about the fact that the same creative concept, the same artistic formula, should have sprung up on the azure coast of Sicily, on the quiet plains of Paestum, in the north, west, south, and east, in the squares of large cities, and in desolate seclusion. For the Greek temple is too universally compelling and abstract not to succeed in adapting itself to any landscape, or rather, in adapting the latter to itself. This constitutes at once the strength and weakness of Hellenic art.

But then, northern architecture always serves to congeal the fragrance of its native fields; it is the child of a particular place and time, of a particular creative moment; it only pulsates in consonance with the surrounding landscape, and to tear the one away from the other is to deal it a deadly blow. When it reaches beyond the confines of its native region, northern architecture immediately turns pale, loses its charm, and thus is deprived of any universally compelling attributes. It does not sustain any formulas or prescriptions for beauty, as it is always prepared to sacrifice the universal for the sake of some overwrought[d] detail.

This naturally results in *the loss of the purity of form*, of self-contained beauty, *the loss of the general clarity of plan and of the clear articulation of the whole into its parts*. Everything is broken up and grouped, or, more precisely, piled up in the fulfillment of a dynamic idea, resulting in a rich and fervent pathos.

The body of an architectural organism then ceases to resemble a rational being, which has as many parts as are necessary, with each one assigned a strictly differentiated function. The work of architecture then proves either to be virtually unarticulated and amorphous, or else to be broken down into the tiniest atoms, which have no independent function other than to embody a collective aspiration subordinated to the basic concept.

The embodiment of the characteristics of northern architecture was already commonplace in the Gothic epoch. Indeed, the grand churches of the style constitute a piling up of small crystals of form, stalactites imbued with straining impulses that disturb and obliterate all the limits, facets, and functions of articulation.

The same characteristics of northern art, however, are even more clearly evident in examples of the northern assimilation of the classical schemes of the south, in specimens of the so-called Northern Renaissance.

In his book on Renaissance architecture, which elucidates the characteristics of Hellenic culture so well, Allesch errs somewhat, in our view, in attributing the same characteristics also to the Italian genius, combining the two under the general term of "Greco-Italian" art.[5]

55

6. It suffices to look at the statue of the Orator in the Archaeological Museum in Florence, at the characteristic features of the sharply outlined individuality [*individuum*], the movement of the hands, whose gesture here constitutes that overwrought detail, that element for which all others are sacrificed, beginning with the Orator's very body, which is concealed beneath the vertical folds of the toga. The Greeks never wanted to conceal the body. The dress covering it emphasized perhaps all the more clearly the outline of the members and their functions. But here in the Florentine Orator the toga deliberately conceals the articulation of the body in order to concentrate the action in an incidental gesture and make it the essence of the entire work. Such are the compositional principles of the majority of the other works of sculpture in Etruria, particularly the astounding figure on the Sarcophagus of Toscanella.

We perceive the essence of "classical" Italian art, which doubtless absorbed an enormous share of valuable aspects from Greek conquests, to be in most respects independent of the Hellenic ideal. Those characteristics that became the unquestionable manifestations of the new, already purely Italic culture emerging in central Italy were a product of many influences, both from the south and from the north and east, melding into the genuinely Italian nucleus that is first encountered in the ancient art of the Etruscans.

It is in Umbria and Etruria and slightly later in Latium and vicinity that we must seek the authentic roots for the classical Italian art that produced such splendid flowerings in the fifteenth and sixteenth centuries.

Etruscan art proved to be short-lived. It survived neither its flowering nor its decline; nor did it achieve the expressive quality that would make it possible for us to regard it as something complete. Still, Etruscan art should not be underestimated because for all its imperfections, it clearly reveals the characteristic aspects of the new, young culture. It is precisely the genetic role of Etruscan art that significantly transcends its self-contained formal significance.

The Etruscans penetrated into the heart of Italy in two colonizing waves from the East (Asia Minor, Lydia) in the fourteenth to the thirteenth and in the eleventh centuries B.C., where, after assimilating themselves into the native population and adapting to the local climatic and living conditions, they created this new Italic nucleus in which southern and northern sources intersected. Even in the modest achievements of Etruscan sculpture we already encounter new characteristics: a strongly manifested predilection for realism and for a portrayal of casual likenesses which breaks through the Hellenic understanding of form.[6]

Turning to Etruscan painting, we can—along with such works as the frescoes in the Corneto Tarquina or the Golini Tomb, where the Hellenic spirit still fully dominates the work of the artist—also point to numerous representations of sorcerers, mimics, harlequins, and acrobats[e] (Tomb of Pulcinella, Corneto Tarquina) which evince altogether new Italic principles. The figures lose their clarity of separation and become merged and dynamic. What emerges out of the resulting treatment of form is not the graphic necessity observed in Greek painting—to emphasize the sense and character of separation—but a newly conceived and altogether painterly sense of life-affirming exuberance, one no longer confined by conventional representations of ideal schemes.

If we turn to architecture, however, we can observe here, more than anywhere else, those characteristic Italic aspects that were conveyed to the Renaissance over the centuries-long span of the Middle Ages.

Appropriating the perfected abstract scheme of the Greeks, the Etruscans adapted it to new social conditions with all the boldness of barbarians who know neither good nor evil. No matter that the perfection was obliterated, for the canonical traditions were breached to make way for new forces that initially proved destructive but that at the same time prepared the ground for future offshoots. The Doric order perfected by the Greeks was monstrously violated: all of its lines became cold and inelegant.

The temple itself, standing on a tall podium with its columns spaced slightly farther apart at the center, contravening the Hellenic scheme in order to satisfy the Etruscans' concrete and real desire to create a more expansive and convenient entrance to the temple, finally attained a desirable sense of scale instead of the abstract modulation devised by the Greeks.

In precisely the same way, we see here the prototype of the classic Italic house with its atrium, loggias supported by brackets or columns, and a pool for collecting rain water (impluvium), which was later transformed into the central fountain of the interior courtyards so favored by Renaissance architects in the fifteenth and sixteenth centuries.

Finally, it is also here that we first encounter on Italian soil the use of the arch and the vault, probably imported by the Etruscans from Mesopotamia, in the sewers, bridges, and monumental gates at Tarquina, Falerii, Sutri, Volterra, Alatri, Perugia, and elsewhere. We likewise note here the first instances in which the arch is integrated into a system of architraved articulation.

Slightly reworked by the Romans a short while later, these conceptions became the constructive and decorative motifs that are indistinguishable from those basic to our own perception of fifteenth- and sixteenth-century architecture.

Having utilized and reworked the aesthetic formulas of the Greeks, the Etruscans naturally could not escape being influenced by individual formal design elements, details, and particularities inherent in the architectural language of the Hellenes.

The primary consequence of all this was that the Etruscan alphabet itself remained Greek. Yet inasmuch as the Etruscans, compared to the Greeks, were barbarians in their utilization of this heritage, these individual elements proved a vulgarization of those in Greek creative work. This is the context in which one should view the "Tuscanian" order of the Etruscans and the Ionic and Corinthian capitals with the naive little palm trees and busts in the center.

The Etruscans barely managed to sow the seeds of their new conceptions. By the beginning of the third century B.C. the Etruscan culture, together with all the stylistic impulses emanating from Greece and the Hellenistic East, was assimilated into the culture of the Romans, who succeeded in developing these established foundations to a higher degree of perfection. Here too, however, the perfection of these new artistic schemes was achieved under the auspices of the cleansing and ennobling influence of the very same Greek images and artists who had increasingly penetrated Roman borders, especially after 146 B.C., the year of the final conquest of Greece.

Thus, the elements of Roman form are undoubtedly products of the same Hellenic culture that lost its purity in the new soil and the new environment.

Yet alongside all this, it is essential to recognize the enormous variety and richness that Roman art attained in the process of applying and integrating these inherited elements of form.

The detached column, standing in a row of other identical columns and with them creating the system of a portico surmounted by a triangular pediment, i.e., the system canonized by the Greek architect, assumed a much more modest role in the life of the Romans. Such columns were retained only in temple schemes, and then only on the front facade, while the entire temple organism was modified according to the conception that had been reworked by the Etruscans (the pseudo-peripteral temple); the remaining three walls of the temple were thus in most instances simply articulated by pilasters or columns partly sunk into the surface of the wall. Such a method might be found in a few Hellenic monuments, of course, but only in an embryonic state. Only with the Romans did this motif achieve a new and far-reaching power. It attained unusual variety and expressiveness in the wall-surface treatment applied to theaters, amphitheaters, and especially triumphal arches.

At the same time, the fact that the columns in the triumphal arch, engaged to the wall surface and seeking to break loose from its hold, produce an uneasy sense of dramatic impact is already indicative of impulses that are wholly alien to the Hellenic spirit and that attain full expression only at the end of the sixteenth century in the Baroque style. This sensation becomes even more expressive when the column, by virtue of its centrifugal pull away from the wall surface, destroys the hitherto smooth, mirrorlike surface of the entablature, projecting its entire vertical profile and breaking it beyond both the line of the cornice and the tall pedestal below the column, as may be seen in a majority of triumphal arches. All this already clearly manifests a new sense of composition, one that is strained, dynamic, and no longer mitigated by the common lines of the entablature and sloping Greek pediment. At the same time, the column is deprived of its constructive function, without which the Greek order is inconceivable. At best, it fulfills a subsidiary role here, resting against the wall and, with it, supporting the overhead load (Basilica Maxentius, the trepidarium in the thermae); in the vast majority of instances, it carries absolutely nothing except a simple or projecting entablature above it (triumphal arches). Thus, the complex sensations that we experience in looking at the Arch of Constantine or the Coliseum in Rome or the arch in Ancona are a result of forces artificially induced on their wall surfaces, a strikingly theatrical dramatization, a kind of purely aesthetic game for obscuring or illustrating their constructive essence, but one always sufficiently self-sustaining and independent to prove a worthy object of view. Here for the first time we vividly encounter in a working construction such a sharp differentiation between the body and the attire clothing it—one that sometimes evolved as a result of the purest artistic invention, of the creative play of fantasy. It thus becomes apparent that in Roman architecture the embodiment of *aesthetic emotion* as such proved as great a goal for the architect as the consideration of any constructive necessity, and that these two aims generally did not coincide, as we saw they did with the Greeks, but rather coexisted alongside and parallel to one another. And though we naturally cannot regard that style which invented a new building material (concrete) and which solved on a grand scale, in a new manner, and with a purely constructive flair the complex problem of roofing spaces with barrel, groin, and domical vaults as an aesthetic style, we nonetheless must recognize the fact that it was precisely Roman architecture that prepared the way for *the already purely aesthetic style of Italy in the fifteenth and sixteenth centuries*, which brought everlasting glory to Renaissance architects.

However, underlying this last word in achievement, proclaimed by the Romans for virtually all the world to hear, was still the same constructive element—the arch and the vault—bequeathed by the Etruscans; and it is here that this element was destined, for the first time, to attain its rightful aesthetic realization.

The use of the arch became commonplace in Roman waterworks. There also oc-

58

curred in Roman art examples of placing an architraved columnar portico in front of a wall with an arched opening, and it is precisely this device that might have supplied a rough outline for the more developed notion of combining these two separate elements—the projecting columnar portico and the arch behind it—on a single surface, thus creating the finished version of a motif that was elaborated so brilliantly in a goodly number of the most varied types of triumphal arches.

It is true that some examples (the gates in Palaiomanina and Palairos) yield evidence that the Greeks had used the arch as well, and that, from the end of the fourth century B.C., there were already numerous instances in which barrel vaults were used in monuments built in Greek settlements (tombs in southern Russia and near Alexandria), while in Ephesus, propylaea have been discovered in which two of the three passageways were arched.[7] It is also possible to find in the Hellenic East and especially in Greece itself (on gravestones on the islands of Delos and Siros) certain embryonic combinations of the arch and the architrave-and-column system that could have served as points of departure for the development of Roman triumphal arches. However, it would be absolutely pointless to conclude as a result that these new artistic devices were affiliated with Hellenic culture. Rather, their existence in this embryonic state, as seen in surviving fragments, speaks even more tellingly of their having been alien to Greek art. For if the Greek architect *knew how* to build an arch, *knew about* combining the arch with the architraved system, *and did not adopt them* as part of his own basic artistic method, then all the more reason that these motifs cannot be regarded as intrinsic to the aesthetic conceptions of the Greeks; at the same time, these motifs emerged as the most characteristic and the most frequently encountered elements of style in Roman art.

The triumphal arches also engendered another architectural device, which was manifested in the exaggerated significance attached to the attics crowning these monuments. Instead of the clear, harmonious scheme for organizing the material of Greek art, we encounter its overstatement in the upper portion of the composition here, and this produces a sense of boundless tension. On the other hand, the integration of the arch with the architraved, columnar portico was also applied to more complex architectural solutions, in which the essential aspects of the same motif were repeated vertically several times, one above the other. The Theater of Marcellus and the Flavian Amphitheater represent the best examples of this device, in which the superimposition of the Tuscan, Ionic, and Corinthian orders one above the other creates parallel bands of rhythmic horizontal and vertical movement. This motif was destined to play a significant role in the conception of the interior courtyards of Italian palaces of the fifteenth and sixteenth centuries; developed on the basis of the old Etruscan atrium with its impluvium and a reworking of the adopted amphitheater scheme, this conception produced such masterpieces of the Renaissance as the courtyard of the Farnese Palace.

Such are the entirely new modes of architectural composition with which Roman art enriched the Hellenic legacy.

The principles of decorative composition, applied to the treatment of both flat and curved surfaces, also underwent a comparable regeneration. Evolving out of Greek decorative schemes, Roman decorative art produced a great number of entirely new compositional methods; the main point, however, is that the very principle of decoration assumed an entirely different character. The decorative

7. K[onstantin I.] Ronchevskii (Ronczewski), *Rimskiia triumfal'nyia arki* [Roman Triumphal Arches (Moscow: Tip. Sablina, 1916). Ronczewski, a professor of architectural history at the Riga Polytechnical Institute and thus someone Ginzburg would have known during his studies there in 1914-1917, authored numerous articles and monographs on ancient Roman architecture and decorative art].

8. K[onstantin I.] Ronchevskii (Ronczewski), *O drevne-rimskikh plafonakh* [On Ancient Roman Decorated Ceilings (1921)].

ornamentation employed by the Greeks, focusing on the sculptural or ornamental frieze, had always been distributed fairly evenly over a surface, creating the degree of smoothness needed to ensure that the decorated surface would not project too abruptly from the general background of the composition. *Harmony*, the prudent and careful distribution of rhythmically pulsating decorative surface areas,[f] had been the basic method of Greek decorative art. The Romans were to take a different approach.

The need to distribute decorative areas along the curved surfaces of the domes and the barrel and groin vaults favored by the Romans had, in itself, compelled the establishment of a system of *primary motifs* (those placed on the least foreshortened areas) and *secondary motifs* (those on greatly foreshortened surfaces). This system thus served to negate the principle that all decorative elements possess equal value. The concept of a centralized surface area in a decorative scheme evolved and was widely implemented, being incorporated in virtually every monument.

The stone slabs of the temple at Palmyra, the vaults of the Arch of Titus in Rome and the Arch of Trajan in Beneventum, the murals of the vaults of the Palace of Nero, and the like are all illustrative of the examples that abound of the emerging new methods of decoration.[8] Although in a majority of instances these centralized surface areas were closely integrated with the overall composition and thus did not disturb the harmonious balance of the whole, they nonetheless caused the eye of the observer to fasten on a particular fragment, as though snatching it out of the whole and forcing the eye to notice and appreciate its exceptional characteristics.

Naturally, all that was new in Roman art was revealed with utmost clarity in the methods by which the architect enveloped space in interiors that were created in an altogether new manner and were disquieting in their ambiguity, as well as in the keenly manifested sense of scale—with the human being as the actual module determining all sizes and dimensions—the impact of which on the observer was comparable not to the effect produced by the clear harmony of the Hellenes, but to that of an awesome and bewildering natural phenomenon.

The abstract genius of the Greek architect had indeed clearly defined the boundaries of three-dimensional space in the longitudinally extended cella, while also creating the very same scheme with clearly expressed functions on the interior, one in which there was nothing accidental or ambiguous.

Now and then, with some reluctance, the Greek architect had resorted to a round form, which possessed less clarity and in which the enclosed space was determined by less certain methods. Even in these rare instances, however, the regularity and small size of the form operated to preserve the orderly and balanced harmony that never abandoned Greek art.

The scale of construction in imperial Rome gave rise to the invention of a new building material—concrete. The use of concrete enabled the Romans to implement with ease the vaulted ceilings required by such an enormous scale: following the domical and the barrel vault, and as the natural culmination of the latter, was the groin vault, which possessed the capacity to define space not centripetally but centrifugally, by creating separate uncoordinated volumes instead of an integral whole. The logical culmination of this conception, and the best example of the new Roman compositional methods, is to be found in the intricate complex of chambers assembled in a new architectural organism—the thermae. The opulence of these monuments, the unprecedented luxury with which these complexes were endowed, and, finally, the place they occupied in the daily lives of the Romans all serve to convince us of the fact that the architectural methods applied here were not a matter of chance, and that, on the contrary, it is here that we must seek the quintessence of the new aesthetic attitudes, conceptions, and aspirations that proved so very unlike the legacy of the Greek genius. Indeed, everything is absolutely differentiated in the thermae. Instead of an integral whole, we encounter a varied complex of rectangular, circular, and square rooms, punctuated by exedras and niches of the most varied configurations, roofed over by flat, decorated ceilings and by barrel, groin, and domical vaults. Instead of the sense of enclosure and clear definition that distinguished Greek conceptions, everything in the thermae is connected by open apertures, arches, and niches: everything flows and moves about without interruption from one volumetric entity to another; everything is ambiguously contained within its boundaries.

Instead of an unvarnished purity and restraint in the application of decorative ornamentation, all of whose elements are always justified by necessity and artistic logic and possess their own rights and responsibilities, as it were, the Roman thermae reveal a richness, brilliance, and complexity in their individual decors; a barbarian, purely Eastern element of variety in their organization; and a desire to assemble all the diverse facets of knowledge and skill in one place, to provide almost more than actually exists.

The restless and belligerent culture of a people striving for continuous conquests, for world hegemony, for pomposity and triumph, was manifested here with unusual clarity and force.

Instead of the cool refinement underlying the Greek methods, there is spirited effort here, a burst of feeling raised to the level of pathos.

Thus, a style that created virtually no new artistic details proved, in its methods of organizing them, in the rhythm of its articulations, in the complexity and richness of its enclosed spaces, and in the great number and variety of its compositional methods, to be a style that was genuinely new, brilliant, and original. Its weak points, in relation to the Greek style, included the presence of *less developed conceptions and the insufficient development of ideas in depth as compared to the considerable breadth of compositional scope*. This latter attribute is of special and particular interest to us, as it is precisely the incompleteness of artistic conceptions that supplied the marvelous, plastic material which the heirs of Rome so avidly assimilated in the fifteenth and sixteenth centuries: something that is incomplete always inspires fertile ideas about potential ways in which it can be completed, thereby supplying vital material for creative work.

The completed and perfected work of art is something consummate and self-contained: it captivates, yet fears any blasphemous contacts. Such was the art of the Hellenes. On the other hand, something that is incomplete always provides greater food for thought by yielding potential opportunities for further development.

Indeed, the Italians of the fifteenth and sixteenth centuries avidly seized upon this very Roman legacy; it was precisely the Roman compositional methods that became a point of departure for Renaissance architects. There does not appear

61

9. Which is easily explained by two circumstances: Milan's location in the northern part of Italy and the participation of foreign masters in the creation of the cathedral.

to have been a single Roman architectural motif that some Renaissance architect did not employ. The captivating Hellenic ideal always remained a perfect and inaccessible paradigm, while the flesh and blood of the Roman ruins wove the living fabric of the Renaissance, becoming increasingly improved and purified, so that for a fleeting moment in history it seemed as though the former Hellenic perfection, pure harmony, and clear and precise compositional method were once more realized with the appearance of Laurana and Bramante.

It is precisely the Roman architectural forms and methods of creative work, as opposed to those of the Hellenes, that we perceive to be the more typically Italian. Here are the very underpinnings of the "aesthetic character" of the Renaissance; here, too, are the sources of its diversity and the richness of its creative scope, culminating in the burst of emotional energy and the powerful surge of pathos that distinguish the period of Italian architecture from Michelangelo to Bernini and Borromini.

There ensued a protracted downfall in the evolution of the forms of classical art. The Middle Ages were shrouded in a dark twilight. The ancient world, having reached its apogee, collapsed under the onslaught of the barbarian tribes. In Europe, northern influence, with all its peculiarities and characteristic aspects, began to prevail once again. The northern barbarians proved incapable of appreciating the brilliant accomplishments of the ancient world, and atop its ruins there gradually arose the impetuous and emotional art of the Middle Ages, at times striking in the amazing boldness and abruptness of its methods, at other times gripping in the all-consuming impact of its pathos.

If the Romanesque style of the Middle Ages is still bound to the heritage of antiquity by its naive vandalization of the latter's elements, the Gothic already represents a self-contained world, an agglomeration of the achievements of the Middle Ages, most forcefully manifesting a different life, a new world outlook, and new ideals, methods, and principles of art. Just as the Greek temple fully reflects the material and spiritual life of the ancient world, so any Gothic cathedral in Europe reflects the whole feudal system, with its theocracy, mysticism, asceticism, and restless, new spirit of mankind.

If in northern Europe the Gothic created its own highly distinctive world of different formal elements and different methods of organizing them, the same, naturally, cannot be said of the Gothic in Italy. Excluding the Milan Cathedral, which, with all its characteristic aspects, constitutes virtually the only example of the Gothic that is fathomable in the European sense of the word,[9] all other monuments dating from this period bear witness to the fact that Italy did not for a minute sever its ties with the ancient traditions, nor for an instant deviate from the influence of the purely Italic classical system.

The cathedrals in Orvieto, Siena, Florence (S. Maria del Fiore, S. Croce), and a multitude of other cities serve best to illustrate this proposition. The Italic[g] Middle Ages had chosen for their churches a facade scheme whose clarity and precision of articulation at once betray the methods of artists schooled in the traditions of the ancient world.

Apparent in all of this art is an inability fully to fathom the new organizational method of the northerners and an unwillingness to relinquish the congenial and comprehensible schemes of the ancient world. The only concessions made are in the details, creating such curious examples as Or San Michele in Florence.

Even more characteristic of the unwillingness throughout most of Italy to accept the Gothic is the strange and captivating phenomenon of the Italian Middle Ages, which blossomed unexpectedly and anticipated by three or four centuries the subsequent sprouting of the Renaissance precisely at a time when the rest of Europe was in the throes of a most impetuous and ecstatic intoxication with the impulsive tendencies of the Gothic style.

This fascinating phenomenon is known in art history as the proto-Renaissance, and its most refined works were created in Tuscany, where the Renaissance itself was subsequently born. The Baptistry and Church of S. Miniato in Florence, together with the Cathedral and Leaning Tower at Pisa, represent the best examples of this art. Here, in contrast to the other monuments of the Middle Ages, we encounter many more elements of antiquity, not only in the basic approach to articulation, but also in the application of individual details. It was not without reason that in the sixteenth century Vasari used the term *rinascita*, applying it to the whole of Italian art beginning in the thirteenth century and even to certain individual monuments of the eleventh and twelfth centuries, and contrasting it to the barbarian art of the Middle Ages.

Thus, we see the classical system of thought, which long ago flowed out of a similar stream, bursting through the barriers of the ages, here and there becoming infused with new energy, and finally, in the fifteenth century, turning into a strong current that gushes out turbulently and majestically.

We perceive this splendid flowering of classical art *not as an unexpected miracle or an incomprehensible return to the ancient past, but simply as the culminating stage in an evolutionary path, as the apogee of this development, a flowering never again to be experienced* and constituting the so-called art of the Renaissance.

Naturally, this art too can only be understood against the background of its epoch, as the consequence of a number of objective factors.

The most formidable barrier that classical art had to transcend was the Middle Ages, with its economic system based on feudal law, creating an endless chain of interdependence and inequality. The need to rationalize this system gave rise to a medieval philosophy (Scholasticism) that imbued feudalism with a sacred character. This accounts for the specific development of the concept of the "kingdom of God," which in turn gave rise to mysticism and asceticism and alienated the architecture of the Middle Ages from life on earth, orienting it upward toward the heavens.

Naturally, such an atmosphere was hostile to the "classical" system of thought in which, on the one hand, the Hellenic world outlook had introduced the clarity and precision characteristic not only of Greek art but of a Greek religion devoid of any mysticism and, on the other, the crude and concrete tastes of the Roman soldier-conquerors could only be satisfied by the flesh and blood of an earthly art. Thus, the subsequent development of the "classical" system could only be realized after the abolition of the most characteristic factors of the Middle Ages.

Indeed, the beginning of the Crusades was accompanied by an increase in trade relations, which destroyed the foundations of a natural economy. Agriculture was divorced from industry, and industry was split up into numerous branches. The result of this entire process was the actual abolition of serfdom and the beginning of an era of social freedom. The revival of trade created an influential class of wealthy townspeople, practical workers to the marrow of their bones, who were wholly occupied by the earthly world and by earthly concerns. Instead of the asceticism that had preached the suppression of feeling, the new tendencies glorified love—a love, moreover, perceived as a true human feeling, passionate and real to the point of crudeness. In the cities, a taste emerged for comfort, for real earthly amenities and benefits. At the same time, a free, integral, and self-conscious personal identity gradually evolved in the cities as well. Trade created a demand for mobility, developed a taste for travel, and revealed as well as broadened the interests and attitudes of the townspeople. The political picture of Italy in the epoch of the Renaissance was one of constant epic struggle: struggle among the different republics, hostilities within the borders of each province between the despot and the bourgeoisie, between the latter and the proletariat (*ciompi*), and between the older and younger guilds (*arti maggiori, arti minori, arti minuti*). It was a struggle that involved and activated absolutely everyone, cultivating personal identity in all its positive and negative aspects; a struggle in which the strongest emerged victorious, although the victor had to be on the alert lest he in turn be conquered.

An individualism developed, although in this instance as a force naturally summoned to life in protest against the centuries-old repression of personal identity—*a fertile and progressive individualism*.

Such were the broad underpinnings for the development of the Renaissance as a style. Even from these few remarks it is clear that the Renaissance could *no longer be satisfied with the forms that had been created by the Middle Ages; that it required its own great, brilliant, eminently workable, and vital art; and that antiquity was merely to be called upon to become a means for the theoretical justification of this art.* Indeed, the ancient system of thought could not have gone further in satisfying such a developing new individualism, one thirsting for its own art in every sense of the word. But then this ancient system as a whole, as an ideology of creative work, as a philosophy and theoretical framework for art, proved exceptionally congenial to the Renaissance, serving as an inexhaustible source of artistic inspiration and as an endless mine of arguments for the struggles and debates which Renaissance theoreticians waged against the Middle Ages.

In other words, *the fifteenth and sixteenth centuries in Italy provided exceptionally auspicious and fertile soil for the subsequent triumphant development of the old "classical" system, summoned to life by new circumstances.* On the other hand, the Middle Ages bequeathed to the Renaissance a guild system of master craftsmen which had worked directly for the consumer over the course of many generations, and in which the artists' guild was in fact a craftsmen's guild. There was no difference between an architect and a master craftsman, and the early Renaissance still abounds in examples of paintings depicting this extremely well-knit collective endeavor. Just as the Gothic architects Jean de Chelles, Libergier, and others were simple workers, so in the epoch of the Renaissance the Sangallo brothers were known as simple carpenters; Rossellino, a simple mason. Brunelleschi was famed as an engraver; Benedetto da Maiano and Pintelli came from a family of specialists in working marble. There was a rule that an architect could not perform his functions until after his acceptance into a corporation of builders; architects could prepare for practice only in a workshop.

The rise of individualism in the Renaissance naturally destroyed this system and crystallized the development of outstanding artists and architects within the rank and file of the guild. To the extent that this individualism was still progressive, so too this crystallization proved to be fertile. The circumstances of the sixteenth century made it possible to construct a history not of architectural monuments, but of individual architects, a fact which marked the culminating point of this crystallization. The subsequent destruction of the guild was disastrous and fraught with unfortunate consequences. A new style of life gradually evolved in which individualism became an aberrant[h] phenomenon. New forms of production were to demand a new approach to art; but more about that later.

Thus, in the epoch of the Italian Renaissance we see, in addition to the general conditions favoring the development of the classical system, the presence of the guild system as well, firmly unified by its sense of consummate craftsmanship. The latter doubtless proved highly significant for the development of style. Inheriting from the Romans and the Etruscans as well as from the Middle Ages an inclination for art firmly rooted in the gamut of local circumstances, the architect-craftsman turned his attention, first of all, to the building materials and conditions for creative work at his disposal. This gave rise to the remarkable and quite distinctive architectural aspects that characterize the different regions of Italy: the richly rusticated aspect of Tuscany, the embossed and incised aspect of Ferrara, the reddish brick aspect of Lombardy and Romagna (Bologna), the marbled aspect of Venice, and so forth.

Only by relying on these different conditions was Renaissance art created, and thereby did the compositional principles of the great Roman architecture, thus transposed, assume a truly exceptional appearance and a distinctive development. Moreover, as had proven the case in Rome, and perhaps to an even greater extent, this art manifested an amazing attribute—*a sense of scale*. Created by and for emergent man and related to the local sense of place, the architecture of this epoch yields examples striking for the strength of their organizational power. Moreover, the object of this organizational energy was not only space itself, enclosed by walls and a roof, but all of the surrounding natural setting as well. The splendid gardens, terraces, and fountains combined with architecture to create an integral whole. Italy's lush, flowering natural setting, on the one hand, and the actual human personality itself for which it all was created, on the other, constituted the two scale modules, the two parameters, within which the architectural conception of the architect was always confidently and precisely integrated, acquiring a most convincing reality and vital integrity in the process. Just as in the democratic Athens of Pericles, so here we encounter two features that fostered the unusual eminence achieved by these arts: the astonishing and, even for these auspicious circumstances, unfathomable outburst of collective genius among the Athenians in the fifth century B.C. and among the Italians in the fifteenth and sixteenth centuries; and the broad social base, exceptional for its time, within which the fruits of this art were disseminated.

But there would be no basis for speaking of a unified "classical" system of European thought were we not also to point out the unceasing influence of the purely Hellenic methods of creative work. Indeed, if, in its individual compositional methods and in the profound sense of reality and scale inherent in its art, the Renaissance proved a direct heir of Rome, then the influence of Hellas should

65

likewise be discerned in its striving for a precision in molding space, for a harmonious completeness of the whole, and for an unrelenting perfection of thought. *The realistic, humanly scaled, and varied art of Rome was filtered through the objectivizing and perfecting prism of Hellas; as a result of such a synthesis, this apex of the "classical" system, its point of culmination, was attained on new ground by new creators.* Architects imbued the reality of each new problem with the kind of clarity and subtlety of organizational thought that could only lead them to a brilliant conception of totally new architectural organisms.

If the Greek architect found the perfect solution for expressing the clarity and authenticity of his spatial experiences in the form of the longitudinally extended rectangular prism, the Renaissance architect turned his attention to another problem, one encountered only episodically in Greek and Roman art—the problem of the centralized spatial volume. Brunelleschi had already advanced numerous solutions to this problem in the Sacristy of S. Lorenzo and the Pazzi Chapel in Florence, but only Bramante's project for St. Peter's in Rome solved the problem of the centralized volume with Hellenic clarity and precision. Placing smaller elements around the dominating volume to balance it in a manner similar to the exact balancing of the two trays on a scale, he defined their interrelationships not just about a single longitudinal axis but about an infinite number of such axes, preserving the vigor of the scheme in every part of the church.

At the same time, compelled by new material needs, the Renaissance architect, instead of adopting either the unified cella of the Greek temple or the disquieting fragmentation of the Roman thermae, learned to divide space into constituent volumes, subordinating them to one another in the expression of a unified conception. What emerged was a clear notion of both the primary elements, which were emphasized, and the secondary ones, which played a subordinate role. In the conception of the house or palace, we encounter an enfilade of chambers, aligned on a common axis and connected by magnificent doorways, enabling the eye to discern their longitudinal progression with absolute clarity. Having adopted the varied system of vaulted ceilings from the Romans, the Renaissance architect rendered them clearly and precisely, in a purely Hellenic fashion. Instead of the disquieting space of the thermae, which extended ambiguously in depth and breadth, we have the palace, where all the opulence and excesses could not undermine the reliability and specificity of the organizational method.

At the same time, this new palace was situated around an interior courtyard in accordance with the same principle of balance evident in the lucid system of the centrally planned church.

Such are the role and significance of the Renaissance as a style. Having completed the hitherto uncompleted art of the Romans with the precision of the Hellene, the Renaissance was able to make a new architectural statement; whereupon, having fully accomplished its mission, it was bound to die. The ensuing development of vital conditions no longer favored the "classical" system. Numerous characteristics that had still appeared progressive in the Renaissance subsequently caused the downfall of the "classical" system.

If something imperfect still remained in classical art, it was the ambiguous and unsettling sense of pathos issuing from many of the works of ancient Rome. The

Renaissance consciously avoided this aspect in its art, seeking to achieve a clarity and authenticity of experience in all its minutest elements and details. To the Baroque, the style that replaced the Renaissance, fell the mission of effecting the final destruction of the classical system, of exhausting this source, a process that has continued virtually to the present day. Here we are confronted with a potent and passionate attempt to master this system, to endow it with unprecedented vitality so that it might regenerate itself. All the means and compositional methods capable of blurring the clarity of defined limits, of obscuring the crystalline forms of space and making their illumination seem ambiguous, are brought into being. A system of contrasts manifested in abrupt changes in perception, a fusion and oversimplified unity in some instances and an excessive agglomeration in others, a tension of rhythmic impulses intensifying and reducing their power—all these are favorite devices of the new style. Finally, the Baroque at times also generated new spatial and volumetric entities; not content with circular rooms, it replaced them with oval ones and continued along this course until it had achieved the most whimsical configurations, which on the whole lie virtually beyond the pale of any architectural method. Nevertheless, in its essence, despite the profoundly new content in the philosophy and taste of the Baroque—the movement and pathos that are already quite familiar to us but that stimulated art with unprecedented power—it simultaneously represents the first serious threat to the great classical system and the last spatial style of architecture, in the broad meaning of the term.

The Baroque was followed in the second half of the eighteenth century by an extended period when the essence of architecture became transformed. The Neoclassical[i] and Empire styles evolved in this period, during which splendid architectural monuments were produced, albeit without spilling any fertile new seeds into the creative lap of the world or breaking any new ground. These styles seemed to be inspired by Rome one day, Greece the next, Egypt the next, then the Renaissance after that, and so on ad infinitum. In essence, this already marks the toppling of the "old" classical system, the downfall of the grandest period in human life.[10]

A thoughtful analysis of the architecture of this epoch will clearly reveal to the investigator that here spatial and volumetric problems receded into the background and the entire work of the architect was channeled into a system of decoration, into details of surface treatment and coloration. These styles, changing quite rapidly during this period without generating any new system of architectural thought, were distinguished from one another merely by systems of decorative articulation, often by details alone. But even these systems were not the products of invention, but merely accommodated and adapted themselves to the times. The character of this essentially decadent epoch is best portrayed by the testimony of those contemporaries who, perennially mired in classical architecture, could never discern its authentic content and, being true to themselves, mined it for nothing more than those decorative schemes and details without which it is impossible to create even the semblance of architecture. Thus, François Benoit, in his treatise on French art at the time of the Revolution, citing some of the aesthetic theories espoused at the time, observes:
"If from the realm of general speculation we turn to practical rules, then we can ascertain that the study of ancient architecture, advocated so energetically and persistently, is reduced merely to a study of the orders. Considered the epitome, the essence of ancient art, the orders become a convenient formula for modern art."[11]

10. It is characteristic that Western Europe never endowed the Empire and Neoclassical styles with as great a significance as did Russia, where they have been studied almost more than the architecture of the Russian north and of Pskov and Novgorod—which naturally possesses a good deal more stylistic significance.
11. [Benoit, *L'Art Français sous la Révolution et l'Empire*, p. 15. See supra, n. 7, chap. 1, for Ginzburg's reference to a Russian translation of this book.]

12. [Ibid., p. 19. Ginzburg's rendering of this quotation fails to indicate that two intervening sentences have been omitted. Ellipsis marks have been inserted in brackets at the appropriate point.]

Later, moving from an elucidation of this conservative theory, as he puts it, to a more progressive one, he persuades us that there was essentially little difference between the two theories. He writes:

"Lacking absolute creativity, a less refined art will be able to achieve relative originality by means of a clever eclecticism, deriving inspiration from all genres, avoiding dissonances, and taking everything that each one possesses which is reasonable or exquisite. [. . .] Thus, the architect will study *ancient art* with a reasoned eye, without any thought of 'servile imitation.' He will only borrow details from the ornamental motifs of antique art, since, on the whole, his architectural system does not correspond to our modern Western needs."[12]

In short, even this aesthetic theory did not advocate the revival of a healthy creativity, but merely sought prescriptions capable of treating the most evident wounds and of creating the illusion of an authentic art.

At the same time, the same eighteenth century and the century following it were fraught with the most crucial developments in the history of mankind. A technological revolution occurred in the period between 1750 and 1850. The steam engine, steam-powered transportation, and mechanized iron production were introduced at this time. These were subsequently followed by the use of electricity, turbine technology, the automobile, and finally aeronautics.

The emerging new building materials underwent a more intensive development, beginning with iron and proceeding to ferro-concrete, the most powerful and stable prerequisites for the conception of a new style. Their appearance served merely as a portent, however, as yet leaving no discernible imprint upon architecture. It merely indicated that new building materials experiencing a rapid technological development and refinement could in no way coexist with the "classical" system of architecture. They had absolutely no need for one another; this, of course, was because the classical system had already long been perfected and, like a saturated solution, could absorb nothing more, while the new elements were, for the time being, compelled to develop independently, being only forcibly and mechanically combined with architecture.

The only natural course open to the architect involved the solution of new problems dictated by the changing conditions of production. The curtain was raised before the architect on the most compelling creative possibilities, which were predicated on a transformed life. However, just as man's attention had to be distracted in the Middle Ages from an actual life filled with oppression, inequality, and subjugation in order to preserve the inviolate feudal system, so too the ascendant class of the sizable capitalist bourgeoisie proved quite indifferent to the prospect of bringing human thought to bear on the authorities [j] in that order. And just as medieval thought and sensibilities were invested with mysticism and the dream of a better world in the "kingdom of God," so, quite naturally, the end of the eighteenth and nineteenth centuries rallied under the banner of a salvation sought in the "classical" system. Here we are speaking not of an effort to find justification in antiquity, but of an unswerving desire to hide from reality, to shield oneself with the impenetrable armor of ancient canons.

To the extent that the nobility and bourgeoisie still constituted a progressive and quite powerful class, the Empire and Neoclassical styles—the last havens for "classical" thought—assumed the trappings of genuine styles: architectural forms, furniture, utensils, clothing, etc., all assumed a single, common tone and complexion, insulating themselves on small isolated islands from the tide of life.

68

It can be said that this last stage was imbued with a luster and a particular beauty. A number of very gifted architects emerged both in this country and in Europe, creating a multitude of incredibly beautiful masterpieces. And yet all this proved useless *from a genetic standpoint*. However handsomely an old man may array himself in elegant attire, he will be unable to produce a new generation. The Empire and Neoclassical styles may have established their own artistic system, but it was merely a system of utilization, a philosophy of reworking one or another of the accessory elements from the culture of antiquity. We shall find here neither a new spatial solution nor any new principles for the organization of mass. No longer could anything new or healthy be extracted from this philosophy, the best intentions notwithstanding. Naturally, this situation could not persist much longer. The twentieth century unfolded with a clear realization of the abnormality of such a situation. The first measures to emerge as a result of this initial discontent proved very troublesome by virtue of the fact that this discontent was still a purely "aesthetic" one, neither willing nor able to penetrate to the heart of the matter. There evolved the highly vulgar "Moderne" and "Decadence" styles, possessing the significance of a repulsive scum on the surface of creative life, subsequently to be cast aside scornfully by the historian. Be that as it may, this scum constitutes, for us, a superfluous commentary on this turn of events: only after the scum is skimmed off the top does the dish become fit for consumption. The essence of the repulsive envelope associated with these new phenomena proceeds, in our view, from its becoming a symptom both of a yearning beginning to be felt for something new, and of a definite onset of weariness with the outlived classical system. Even healthy concepts of the honest expression of new building methods and materials proved to be vague and undeveloped. However, all this was hardly realized at the time and reflected more the impotence of the old than the significance of the new, leading to the creation of superficial and contrived forms incapable of sustaining any hope for their more or less prolonged life. These styles, which did not create a single monument of the slightest significance, quickly faded away, giving rise to a natural reaction.

In the decade prior to the war there flourished in Petrograd and other Russian cities a galaxy of highly gifted architects who took this thankless mission upon themselves. By virtue of their great skill, high culture, and creative energy a rather significant number of well-composed and well-articulated monuments arose in a relatively short period of time, even managing to create the impression of some sort of flowering of architecture. Yet, the latter impression proved a false one, and for all the talents possessed by these masters, the matter did not extend beyond the level of the most idiosyncratic kind of eclecticism.

In less than a decade, these architects began to rush for help to Michele Sanmichele, Serlio, Palladio, Scamozzi, or to a host of leading exponents of Russian Neoclassicism; moreover, the artistic taste of these architects, for all their sophisticated skill, could at times be satisfied by an almost literal replication of the more typical palace schemes and, in the best of circumstances, their adaptation to different situations. If we add the fact that the creative work in question still assumed the character of a phenomenon utterly divorced from life, then the entire matter, in our view, acquires a particular complexion. The high level of workmanship apparent in individual monuments, the lack of principle and the rapid and frivolous fluctuation of ideals, and the rarefied sense of culture and refinement in art all constitute well-known indications of the decline of a style, the last steps of a once-triumphant procession.

At this point Europe endeavored, albeit not very successfully, to come up with new forms of architecture. Italy, though closest to the center of the Greco-Italic system, nonetheless created monuments of astounding triteness and banality. Also rather unsuccessful were the achievements of France, another Romanic country, which sought to retain the nationally reworked classical system in its creations. The northern countries, including England, did not go beyond the development of purely indigenous types of cottages and small buildings in general, which derived their primary significance from the generally evolving concept of village construction. Finally, Germany attempted, with typically German awkwardness, to create an austere monumental style, fusing a simplified classical system with indigenous motifs.

Such is the general picture of European architecture in the nineteenth and early twentieth centuries, a picture that, as we can see, is a rather dismal one, leading many pessimists to entertain somber thoughts about the general downfall of architecture.

But if Europe, with its vast size, presents a picture of complete decline, America, primarily the United States of North America,[k] offers a more instructive view.

A new national power that has not yet had the time to accumulate its own traditions and artistic experience quite naturally turns to Europe for assistance; Europe, true to the stodgy ideals of its classical system, begins transporting its products across the ocean. However, the life of North America as a vital new power cannot, despite its own wishes, proceed along a course well trodden by other cultures. An American tempo of life is emerging, utterly different from that of Europe—businesslike, dynamic, sober, mechanized, devoid of any romanticism—and this intimidates and repels a placid Europe. Nevertheless, wishing to be "as good as" Europe, America continues to import European aesthetics and romanticism as though they were commodities that had stood the test of time and been "patented," as it were. Thus, there emerges a single aspect of America: a horrifying mechanical mixture of new, organic, purely American elements with the superficial envelopes of an outlived classical system "made in Europe." The frightful forty-story Renaissance marvels and other similar nonsense perpetrated by the young America have already been judged, seemingly by everyone, on their own merits.

Yet at the same time, in those instances when the American genius permitted itself the luxury of doing without Europe's help, when the crude and sober but nonetheless potentially vigorous spirit of the new pioneers manifested itself, brilliant structures teeming with unexpected poignancy and force were created spontaneously in an absolutely organic manner. I have in mind the industrial structures of America, and we shall have more to say about them later.

The America emerging at the beginning of the twentieth century thus generally presents a rather different picture. Along with the downfall of the classical system, we see flashes of a new idea, though for the time being not in "art" but in utilitarian buildings whose role and significance transcend the structures themselves.

Thus, the cycle of the "classical" Greco-Italic and, in a certain sense, European system of thought appears, to us, to have been completed, and the path to a genuine modern architecture must surely lie beyond it. Does this mean that the whole complex path taken in the course of the centuries-long development of European architectural thought has proven to be "superfluous," and that we shall be forced to begin our own creative work at the very beginning, outside of and beyond the completed cycle?

Of course not. In the first place, we simply *cannot do so*, just as a person cannot leap over himself, and an abrupt change in the primordial foundations of human thought and perception—and, hence, in the creative work that concerns us—is physiologically impossible.

The system of spatial experience developed in Europe over the centuries is something that is intrinsic not only to the modern architect, but to any mortal as well, as is the case with any other aspects or conventions of cultural life. In the second place, however, *we do not even wish to do so*, just as we do not wish to forsake any other achievements of past cultures that have objectively been deemed to be of value.

The question thus remaining to be answered is this: which aspects of this completed cycle of architectural life can be regarded as possessing such value? Which parts of the whole artistic and historical baggage should we pursue with not only dispassionate appreciation, but the unrelenting perseverence of a modern, vitally concerned human being as well?

Naturally, this question concerns neither the elements of any style nor their formal characteristics, but rather those basic *philosophical and architectural profundities* whose power has not yet abandoned us.

At issue here are two contradictory sources of architectural thought, hurling us alternately into the currents of different stylistic tendencies.

One of them, that of the South, first achieved its perfected development, as we saw, in the architecture of Hellas. Briefly formulated, this development was distinguished by the *purposive clarity of the spatial solution, which attained its formal expression in the form of longitudinally extended organisms. The Italian art of the fifteenth and sixteenth centuries devised* an expression of the same well-defined spatial experience in the form of *centrally planned architectural organisms*. These it rendered in intricate architectural complexes and multifarious structures, *combining the system of longitudinal expansion with the closed, centralized system.*

In both Greece and the Italian Renaissance, we encounter *a precise articulation of the whole into parts and a harmonious coordination of these parts, resulting in the internal balance and decorum that distinguish these two modes of architecture.*

In this sense, the Hellenic flowering and the Italian Renaissance each represent styles that display a particular aspect of the European genius with remarkable authority.

The other source, manifested most brilliantly in *the Gothic and the Baroque*, introduced different characteristics while utilizing the same basic organisms; these characteristics can be seen in the *predilection for dynamic aspects and for a pronounced sense of movement, investing perception not with a calming ef-*

71

fect, but with the impulsive and unsettling feeling of pathos.

Instead of encountering the harmonious moderation of an ordering and organizing spirit, we collide in these styles with *an impulse that sweeps all precisely defined limits aside and creates entirely different compositional methods.*

These two systems of architectural thought comprise that part of our cultural heritage which is still adequate to satisfy the needs of modernity.

Which one is the more congenial to us? Both are. This constitutes the source of their genetic significance, of their potential value for the present day.

The *purposive clarity* of the spatial solution—is this not the source of modern *rationalism*, of the attention we so carefully devote to the precise articulation of the utilitarian problem?

Dynamics and its penetrating force—are these not the elements of modern artistic impact, are they not the attributes that are most avidly pursued by present-day architects?

The consolidation of this at first glance seemingly contradictory heritage—*the purposive clarity of the spatial problem, materialized and invigorated by the power of movement*—does this not constitute the legacy of modern creative work with which we too are now entering upon a new cycle in the development of European artistic thought?

It need hardly be said that the essential terms for expressing this new cycle have yet to be discovered; they reside in the new life surrounding us which we long did not wish to recognize. Blending elements of the old life and the new, they encompass the essence of that law of continuity about which we spoke in the preceding chapter.

These landmarks, as they acquire a new language of expression, will be enriched by a new world of experience, in whose mainstream the new style is long destined to thrive. Thus regeneration will continue until such time as, at a particular moment in history, the investigator will be confronted with an orderly and perfected new system of creative work, one bearing no resemblance whatever to classical thought, and independent of it. This will mark the fulfillment of the new style, its long-awaited flowering. All that, however, still lies fully ahead.

3.
The Prerequisites of
the New Style

Steam cooler for the Tissen machine factory

A new style does not emerge all at once. It begins in various facets of human life, which frequently are totally unrelated to one another. The old is regenerated gradually; frequently one can observe how elements of the old world, still persisting by reason of traditions that have outlived the very ideas which engendered them, coexist side by side with elements of the new world, which overwhelm us with their barbaric freshness and the absolute independence of their unexpected appearance. However, the new elements manage, on the strength of their vitality and purely organic legitimacy, gradually to entice more and more facets of the old world until, finally, nothing can stem the tide. The new style becomes a fact, and those refusing to accept that fact condemn themselves to a complete and grievous isolation: no homage to past cultures can alter the situation; the world, steeped in its bold sense of legitimacy, recognizes only itself. This provides the key to its creative power and to the triumph of its march of conquest.

Producing such an analysis of the evolution of style is certainly far easier for the investigator—for whom artistic monuments and historical and cultural materials pertaining to the epochs under study appear in a historical perspective cleansed of any biases of the day and aftertastes of personal involvement—than for the contemporary wishing to justify and validate the new world of which he feels himself to be a part.

General view of the Ansaldo airplane factory in Turin

However, there are certain circumstances which make it easier for one who is both contemporary and investigator in this respect and which thus facilitate the solution of this problem.

The World War and the Russian Revolution, which assumed the role of a grandiose cataclysm that shook and toppled the foundations not only of our own native land but also of the world at large, were events that, in their sweep and the burst of psychic energy unleashed each step along the way, drew a sharp boundary line between the old and the new; they played a role no less profound than had proved the case in any other period of historical displacement, cleansing the horizons and facilitating the crystallization of a new and more viable culture.

Thus, what prior to the war and revolution might have appeared even to the discerning eye to be a momentary weariness now stands out clearly and indubitably as something that is assuredly a thing of the past and dying off. All these events, like a deafening blow, jarred many seemingly immovable foundations and rescued us from the abyss of the myriad habits and conventions that had supplanted the effective energy of creation.

The significance of the events that led to this change makes it possible to survey the picture of the past virtually from a historical vantage point, removing the veil from our eyes and providing us with an opportunity to render a deliberate assessment of the situation. Standing vividly before us at the present time are, on the one hand, a number of elements of the new life which lay hidden prior to the cataclysm and which we then had all but overlooked, but which now emerge before our eyes as the principal factors of the new world, and on the other hand, a number of gods and idols whose splendor, proving empty and false, has disintegrated like superfluous rubbish.

A new culture is almost always summoned into being by the appearance in the historical arena of a new nation, nationality, or social group that up until that time has languished as if in a state of lethargic sleep or infancy, thereby preserving its creative forces and able to pour youthful juices into the decrepit body of mankind. Arising out of an extended passive existence and becoming a more active element in creative life, this new effective factor imbues creative energy with the characteristic features and peculiarities of the environment from which it has evolved. Thus, the Dorians inevitably brought with them, along with their virile origins as conquerors, a number of purely northern traits which were retained in the new circumstances of life by virtue of tradition, but which nonetheless became firmly established and long retained their power.

Such, very likely, was the case with the gable roof of the Doric temple, which evolved as a result of climatic conditions more severe than those in most Greek settlements, but which remained a formal element of the basic Greek style even in the southernmost regions of the Hellenic world. Along with the new designer of precious objects, a new consumer also emerged out of this same environment in which the gable roof motif had become such a desirable element of form, quite irrespective of its constructive and utilitarian significance. In this way, a new creative environment gives rise to formal elements whose significance is magnified and applied to a far wider range of design objects. The gable roof motif was applied to virtually all Greek monuments; we find it in temples, propylaea, and porticos, even though it was no longer engendered by the organic conditions of life. Such is the role of a new environment that embarks upon a course of active creation.

In precisely the same manner, the process of creating a new social environment—the class of merchant townspeople—begun in the Middle Ages and lasting for several centuries summoned to life a creative force that was destined to destroy the decaying feudal order. The townspeople were totally overwhelmed by the earthly world, by earthly matters, faith, and the significance of a revived sense of individualism, which obliterated the significance of the theocracy and asceticism that had been the mainstay of the Middle Ages. Just as the elements of the Doric roof had gradually been applied over an increasingly greater area of the Hellenic world, so too the new world outlook developed by the townspeople did not remain their exclusive domain. This crystallization of new thought continued for a number of centuries, leading to the development of an urban art, a purely civil architecture, which reached its flowering in the fifteenth and sixteenth centuries. And quite analogously, these new elements of a townspeople's art acquired a significance that led to their being applied to all manifestations of creative work of the period.

Turning now to modernity, we cannot fail to note the new social element that gradually is penetrating more fully into life and that unquestionably is destined to play that role of a rejuvenating force which has always emerged in the historical arena at times such as these. No wonder the problem of workers' housing has become the most characteristic problem of modern architecture, not only here in Russia but throughout Europe as well. The presence of a new social consumer of art is evident. He is increasingly attracting the architect's attention and gradually generating new demands and new architectural problems that require a different creative approach. It is imperative that we consider those aspects of the active new consumer environment which possess the greatest creative potential and which, on the strength of the aforementioned law, permeate all manifestations of creative life, even those whose organic link to that environment may not be so readily apparent.

Each historical period, or rather each vital creative force, is characterized by certain artistic organisms; each epoch in the plastic arts thus has its favorite types, which are especially characteristic of it—such as, for example, the frontal type of Archaic statues, endowed with a particular smile, which was repeated during a certain epoch of Hellenic art as single-mindedly as was the particular image of the Madonna subsequently developed and established by some artist of the Renaissance. Precisely the same phenomenon applies to architecture as well. The temple, with its typical features, is thus most characteristic of Greece, the church and cathedral of the Middle Ages, and the palace of the Renaissance. This does not mean, however, that the aforementioned organisms exhaustively characterize the given epochs; it simply indicates that the artists' main energies were directed toward solving these particular problems, and that the forms created in the process assumed paramount importance in the minds of their contemporaries, and were transferred not so much organically as consecutively to other aspects of creative endeavor. Thus, the scheme devised by the Greeks for the temple organism was readily transferred to all the other building types of the period. Likewise, the elements of Gothic architecture which predominated were transferred to the civil architecture of the period (town hall, communal house[a]), while conversely, in the Renaissance, the formal elements of civil architecture were transferred to church organisms on the strength of already modified aesthetic ideals.

The element of life that has been thrust to the forefront of the vital new social environment of modernity—the working class—is *labor*, inasmuch as it represents the main content of the life of that environment, its unifying symbol.

The concept of the value of human labor, however crude and primitive it might be, the concept of life as heroic toil, the poetry of the hammer and anvil as the basic elements of physical labor—all these aspects have surfaced in certain works of art in the preceding decades, sometimes yielding highly significant paradigms. Now, even more, free and joyous labor has become, in our view, one of the most striking manifestations of human existence.

To labor—its force and power, its energy—and to all the realms of active life that it encompasses, we are unhesitatingly prepared to devote our best artistic potentialities.

Thus moving to the forefront as the basic task confronting modernity is the development of solutions for all the architectural organisms associated with the concept of labor—*workers' housing and the house of work*—and for all the innumerable problems generated by them.

Hence, the logical conclusion, based on an analysis of historical developments, is that these problems will, in their signification, outgrow themselves, and that the elements generated by their solution will become the basic elements of an altogether new style.

Long before the war the problem of workers' housing had already been thrust to the forefront by life. The increasing number of workers associated with the various rapidly growing segments of capitalist production presented the government or the owners of these enterprises with the need to create housing that would stimulate and to some extent assure the availability of the work force needed for production. Thus, a significant number of workers' settlements is to be found in Europe at the present time. The extent to which this problem has been thrust to the forefront by life is demonstrated by the characteristic development wherein a competition for standardized workers' housing organized in 1918 under government auspices by the Society of British Architects[b] drew eight hundred competitors and amassed 1,738 projects (none of which, incidentally, were very interesting from a qualitative standpoint). Much has been done by other countries as well, including Russia, where the latest competition sponsored by the Moscow Architectural Society has produced a series of projects that compare favorably with those of Europe. However, the essence of these numerous solutions, both those which have been implemented and those which have not, naturally reflects not a feeling for new form, but an absolute dependence on past cultures, one that emanates from the interpretation of housing as a palace or a detached house defining the basic problems of housing and leaving its mark on the stylistic character of workers' housing. All the existing solutions in this latter category represent, aesthetically speaking, the same Russian detached house or English cottage in which economic considerations alone prompted the reduction of floor space. What we unquestionably have here is not workers' housing as such, but ordinary housing for an economically disadvantaged segment of the population. The hypocrisy and aesthetic deception of such a solution, with its incredibly naive reduction of the scale of the nineteenth-century manor house, is especially apparent when one compares this solution to any of the actual manifestations of modern life. A small, low house with isolated entrances and exits, its own outbuildings, small kitchen, flower gardens, and other delights, located on a maximum of several dozen square arshins[c]—is this ideal, which is earnestly being proposed for the worker even now, not the one embraced by the sentimental and individualistic bourgeoisie in the past?

It must be realized that workers' housing that is *modern* in its standard mode of formal expression is a problem whose solution still wholly lies ahead. Everything that has been erected to date in this regard constitutes an aesthetic legacy of the old culture. Still, even in these imperfect efforts it is possible to discern tendencies that, insofar as they come into contact with aspects of the new life, are destined to go into the melting pot of the new. Even in the sentimental small houses of the garden city, we can already see a gradual *liberation from the formal elements of the obsolete classical system* (it is difficult to find a worker's house now with columns in the Empire style) *and the penetration of plain, unconcealed construction and of the rational utilization of space by a logical simplicity;* moreover, to the extent that these small houses are always conceived as part of a general ensemble, as part of the process of planning an entire collective, the individualistic aspects of the detached house are localized, and there arises an idea of communal needs. Finally, we come to organized building production and its standardization. Even in these initial steps we encounter *a spirit of collectivism, a range of architectural scale that impels an austere and energetic expression.* We naturally have no concrete idea what future workers' housing will be like, but it would not be risking too much to predict that it is these very characteristics, engendered by the characteristics of *workers' housing as such*, that will provide the basis for it.

The manifestation and formation of an authentically modern workers' way of life, which thus far has changed little and which we can envisage only to a certain extent, will determine the remaining unknowns as well; only as a result of this process will it be possible to define this still vague ideal.

If the aesthetic problem of human housing and, by extension, workers' housing is still rather far from being solved, then, on the other hand, the other requirement claimed by labor—the *house of labor*, the factory, the plant, the industrial facility—is undoubtedly in much better shape. Naturally, the explanation for this situation is not very difficult to find. Very few forms of human existence advance at the same pace in the course of their development. The more sensitive elements are modified more rapidly, yielding to new forms of life, while the remaining elements continue steadfastly to preserve the continuity of tradition. Man's way of life, that worldly atmosphere which encompasses his daily existence and does not directly reflect the harsh and implacable struggle for survival—the most active facet of his life—has always been a highly conservative element. The form of domestic utensils and the character of residential interiors and of dwellings in general usually continue to wear out the forms from the preceding epoch, while the methods and techniques of waging war or tilling the soil, for example, being more expedient, already bear the stamp of modernity. A new cannon or the model for a battleship or textile loom always changes its aspect far more rapidly than do the forms and styles of the bed on which a person sleeps—not to mention the already exceptional conditions of modernity by virtue of which almost every new product of a machine factory is different from the preceding one in its constructive aspect. Hence, it is only natural that a solution in the modern sense to the problem of human housing will come much later, at a time when the new conception of style becomes so pervasive that it fills all the corners of human existence, when the new man's way of life becomes manifestly crystallized, a way of life which for the moment is flowing archaically down a long-since dried-up riverbed.

Thus, in order to clarify the point that concerns us, it is necessary to refer to other organisms that are linked more directly to the process of labor. It is perfectly natural that the problem of the *house of labor—of industrial structures—* as the outpost of modern life should yield more exhaustive data than the problem of workers' housing; indeed, we are now already aware of the countless number of extraordinarily superb European and American structures in which a vigorous eruption of modernity has yielded solutions that are astonishing in their purely formal perfection, unquestionably foreshadowing what is to come. Hence, it is easy to understand why it is precisely these industrial structures that, in our primordial epoch of the crystallization of style, should serve as those model organisms that will provide us with a point of departure for the continued development of architecture.

Indeed, modern industrial plants condense within themselves, in an artistic sense, all the most characteristic and potential features of the new life. Everything capable of establishing the essential thrust of creative progress is to be found here: a picture of modernity that is extremely lucid and differentiated from the past; endless silhouettes of the forcefully moving muscles of thousands of arms and legs; the deafening roar of orderly monster-machines; the rhythmic operation of pulleys, uniting everything and everyone with their movement; the rays of light penetrating the taut veil of glass and steel; and the collective output

80

of valuable products extruded from this creative crucible. Can there be a picture that more clearly reflects the purposeful way of life of modernity?

However, if one were to think about what actually gives this image its vividness and tension, one would easily realize, of course, that it is first and foremost the *machine*. Take the machine away from the modern factory and you will immediately see the loss of that rhythm, that organization, and all that pathos of labor. It is precisely the machine, the main occupant and the master of the modern factory, which, having already exceeded its bounds and gradually filling all the corners of our way of life and transforming our psyche and our aesthetic, constitutes the most important factor influencing our conception of form. For this reason, we shall permit ourselves to dwell in somewhat greater detail on an analysis of its attributes and peculiarities and its characteristic aspects.

An essential feature of any society that exists at a significant cultural level, a feature decisively affecting all forms of human activity and therefore art as well, is the nature and interrelationship of its productive forces. Thus, the question of the means of production operating in a given epoch acquires particular importance and significance from our point of view. There is no longer any doubt about the role and consequences of the changeover from stone to iron weapons for all realms of human activity, including that of art; equally apparent to modern art historians is the dependence of the broadly unified style of the Egyptian plastic arts dating from the early periods upon the organic methods of working the material then at the Egyptians' disposal. And yet the greatest upheaval in the life of man, produced by the appearance and promulgation of the machine as a new and powerful means of production, is utterly ignored by investigators of art. As if, when it comes to modernity, it were possible to change a causal relationship that always has been discernible in human society! As if it were possible to suppose that this highly perceptible change in technology could remain detached from the development of art, particularly of architecture, whether the modern art historian and artist want this or not!

The machine, which emerged as a result of the inventiveness of human genius in its struggle for material well-being and satisfaction of purely utilitarian demands, has for some time now been a part of our lives. Given that it appeared and began to spread precisely at a time when notions of "utility" were perceived to be diametrically opposed and even harmful to "aesthetic" conceptions, the role that the machine and the forms issuing from it have assumed in our artistic world outlook is thus a perfectly natural one. It would not be wrong to say that the machine, in our conception of it, was the apotheosis of the triteness and vulgarity of the real world, its unfortunate inevitability, something which the artistically cultivated person scrupulously avoided. The machine and the engineering construction associated with it were regarded as the antithesis of the work of art, particularly of architecture, just as the epithet "constructor" was used in opposition to the term "architect." There was an unbridgeable gulf between engineering and architecture; in joint undertakings, the architect and engineer were hostile and always remained incomprehensible to one another.

We all still remember those poetic and rather sentimental yearnings for idyllic rides in stage coaches and post chaises, the genuine disgust we experienced at seeing railroads and funiculars plough through the virgin landscape of the Alps and Pyrenees, and the deep despair we felt at having the urban ensemble spoiled by the intrusion of modern bridges and the bleak silhouettes of industrial buildings. In a word, we were opposed to modernity; if the artist had been able to control fate, he surely would not have hesitated to seize every opportunity to stop this menacing invasion of the machine.

Now, however, all this seems rather dated and naive. The machine, quite impervious to the scorn heaped on it by the artist, continued on its march of progress. With each succeeding year, its numbers steadily increased. It began penetrating all the pores of our way of life, our lives, and positively disrupting all our aesthetic ensembles. Not content with having cut up mountains, valleys, and forests, having tamed the urban landscape, and having moved from the streets to the interiors of buildings, the machine extended its reach still farther, penetrating into the most god-forsaken corners. Finally, it committed the ultimate sacrilege by defiling the azure blue of the sky, which up until that time had remained unspoiled and the exclusive domain of poets. For the aesthete, this became an intolerable situation and no laughing matter. No longer was there any place left to hide from the machine; the natural course of events foreshadowed its continued march of progress, thereby finally making it necessary to reckon with it one way or the other. To have cast all thoughts of the machine aside in complete isolation even from man's artistic activity would have been to risk winding up along the sidelines, isolated from life in general. For art, and especially architecture, is naturally incapable of leading an existence cut off from economics and technology, as well as from the landscape, way of life, and human psychology.

The machine summoned to life the factory that gives it substance and the engineering structures that are its consequence; together they establish a new character for the city. Is it possible for a work of architecture existing in this mechanized life to remain an archaic enigma despite all the laws of creativity and style, despite all the conclusions that can be drawn from an analysis of the history of the arts? Certainly not. Indeed, the artist's attitude toward the machine has itself been undergoing change. It is possible to detect approximately three periods in this process.

The first period, filled with hostility and an aesthetic rejection of the new manifestations of life, dates from the time when machines and engineering structures first appeared, when the artist, if he came into contact with them at all, did so merely to conceal and mask the new face of life through the artifice of his artistic skills. It was a period when factories were built in the "Empire" style and splendid bridge trusses were adorned in the "Renaissance."

The second period occurred not long before the war, when the machine and the new way of life that it engendered began calling greater attention to themselves, when the significance of this new life began dimly to be felt. The architect's work in this new period was split up into two realms: the architect no longer quite had the audacity to distort the engineering aspect of industrial structures with traditional forms; but then in the realm of public and domestic architecture, he compensated himself for these deprivations. A multitude of magnificent bridges, factories, and all sorts of machines appeared, still independent of "art," although their self-contained perfection was already sensed by many. The wonderful machine began to inspire a sense of awe whose disposition would have been revealed, upon careful scrutiny, to be rather far removed from the earlier hostility.

Finally today, now that war and revolution have enhanced our vision, now that the reevaluation of old concepts has become a commonplace, we are entering into the third period, one in which the machine has assumed an entirely different role in our lives. We are on the eve of an already distinctly formulated and purely modern understanding of form, one in which the dichotomy of the second period must disappear, in which we shall have the audacity to set as our task the ultimate architectural ideal—the creation of a genuinely harmonious art, a harmoniously constructed ensemble of life in which everything is permeated with the genuine rhythm of modernity. *The machine, which we initially scorned and from which we subsequently attempted to isolate art, now finally can teach us to build this new life.*

What ensemble are we talking about? Is it the ensemble of the Americanized capitals of the world, or that of the quiet landscape of the Russian provinces and countryside, whose way of life still has not progressed appreciably beyond that of the eighteenth century?

Are we correct in asserting that it is necessary to build on the urban front, so striking in its modernity, rather than in those remote areas of our native land that life has passed by? Of course we are, for it is important to establish both the nature of the process and its direction in order to know how to orient our actions. If certain immutable organic laws of growth have become widely recognized, then, rather than obstruct them, it is much more reasonable to adapt to them and to master them.

No matter what our predilections, life sooner or later will demand that we provide even the countryside with electric power, supply it with a multitude of various machines, dot its quiet plains with tractors, and enliven its horizons with elevators. That this must come to pass is *indisputable* and something that no one can deny; consequently, here too, even in building the countryside, we have far greater cause to emulate an ensemble that, though as yet non-existent, is far more inevitably a thing of the impending future than some style of the eighteenth century. Naturally, the distinctions between life in the country and life in the city, between one place and another, one locality and another, will all surely be reflected in architecture, will imbue it with a particular aspect, and will distinguish one nationality from another. But this differentiation, despite its fundamental significance, does not concern us at the present time. We now must proceed on the basis not of specifics, but of those general and crucial aspects that can synthetically be discovered in Europe, in America, in the noisy city, and in the quiet province, all of which are equally subject to the same inevitable laws of development. It is not surprising, therefore, that the ensemble we are speaking about at the present time is the ensemble of the largest modern cities of Europe and America.

Local and national characteristics in the present instance appear too insignificant when compared with the equalizing force of modern technology and economics.

4.
The Machine.
The Influence on Modern Art of
the Static and Dynamic
Properties of the Machine

Machine and transmission

One of the fundamental characteristics of the machine as an independent organism is its extraordinarily well-defined and precise *organization*. Indeed, a more distinctly organized phenomenon can hardly be found in nature or in the products of human effort. There is no part or element of the machine that does not occupy a particular place, position, or role in the overall scheme and that is not the product of absolute necessity. There is not and cannot be anything in the machine that is superfluous, accidental, or "decorative" in the sense conventionally applied to habitation. Nothing can be either added to or taken from it without disrupting the whole. What we encounter in the machine, essentially and primarily, is the clearest expression of the ideal of harmonious creation, which long ago was formulated by the first Italian theoretician, Alberti.[1]

The machine demands of the constructor an extraordinarily precise expression of concept, a clearly realizable goal, and an ability to articulate a scheme into separate elements related to one another by an indestructible chain of interdependence, with each element constituting an independent organism that clearly manifests the function for which it was made and to which all its aspects are subordinated.

As in other realms of human activity, the machine above all impels us toward *utmost organization in creative work and toward clarity and precision in formulating a creative idea.*

Airplane manufactured by the Ansaldo factory

However, in view of the fact that each element of the machine derives its meaning as a function of both a particular and a general necessity, and given that these necessities vary with each change in a machine's aspect and that there is an endless number of these aspects, the constructor must be a creator from start to finish, inventing for each machine its own elements and its own scheme for integrating them—in short, its own distinctive harmonious principle. Thus, the machine, which engenders an impulse within us for purely harmonious activity, prevents that activity from becoming hardened into a canon by imbuing it with variety and inventiveness. This constitutes that aspect of harmonious creativity whose laws, while precise and immutable for each separate organism, lose their power when transferred to another organism, which requires the active construction of its own new harmonious scheme.

It is not difficult to convince ourselves of the fact that this transition from creative impressionism to a clear and precise construction, one which represents an exact response to a firmly postulated problem, is a phenomenon now becoming common to all forms of human activity.

With each passing day, science's march of progress bears ever new fruit from this clear and deliberate activity, which has come to replace various and sundry idealistic ambiguities.

In precisely the same way, the "mysterious" mission of the artist, whose motive power has been no less "enigmatic," must be more firmly and deliberately grounded. The artist must move from the cloud-transcending heights of Olympus down to the harsh, real world, drawing nearer to the craftsman, who is always faced with distinct and clearly defined problems. From the machine, the genuine artist will again learn the art of articulating his conception into separate elements, binding them to one another in accordance with the laws of inviolable necessity, and finding an exactly corresponding form for them. Instead of fortuitous, impressionistic impulses, the artist will have to develop an ability to deal with his aspirations and to strengthen them within the bounds of what is possible for each realm of art and for each material—an ability to find the precise limits of his conception. In all these efforts to bring creative work down from false and grandiloquent heights to the domain of sensible laws of organization lies the promise of this vigorous and bracing force. Its convergence with the monotonous, everyday manifestations of life, its prosaicness, represents that genuine reality of art, that concreteness of its formal language, which will enable it to be saved from the great danger that threatens modern art— abstractness.

A number of other qualities likewise emanate from the machine's orderly organization. Indeed, since the constructor's goals are organized with such conceptual clarity, it is natural that his inventiveness should not cease until a material has been found that corresponds to the necessary element, until that element obtains its most concise expression, and until its form assumes a profile that assures its most economical movement in the combined overall system. Hence, the search for precisely that material which best fulfills the designated function, and the endless search for a form for each joint, valve, or piston until the simplest and most perfect solution is found. Thus, under the influence of the machine *is forged in our minds a concept of beauty and perfection as entities which best respond to the characteristics of the material being organized and to its most economical utilization in the realization of a specific goal, one which is the most condensed in form and the most distinct in movement.*

This already constitutes a complete philosophical system of creativity, the result of which is that it is no longer possible to be indifferent to the materials at the architect's disposal or to perpetuate the "plaster" styles of the nineteenth century, in which surfaces of plaster were molded in imitation of various kinds of materials. The architect made wiser by the ways of the machine is now confronted by the complex problem of choosing materials or, if there is no such choice, the even more difficult problem of adapting to existing ones. The rational organization of the latter is the architect's most important task. The modern architect will not cover a material with a coat of plaster, but will expose it as clearly and forthrightly as possible, exploiting and emphasizing its properties. For all the modern style's commonality of language, the most diverse variations of it will appear, such as the style of wood or of concrete, the style of glass and iron or of ferro-concrete; for the architect's task, like that of the constructor of the machine, involves not arbitrary improvisation but a reasonable organization of the material at his disposal. In this work, moreover, the careful economizing of the energy of the material will become a perfectly natural phenomenon. For the whole purpose of the architect's organizational power derives from the reasonable utilization of the "work" performed by the material. Hence, the material that "does not work," that does not perform some function in one sense or another, will be useless and superfluous, and thus will have to be removed from the composition. In this way interrelationships will be established among all the parts, supports, and bearing and non-bearing elements as functions of suitable materials, of the work assigned to them, and of their effective energy. Harmony must come into being not through a lifeless scheme executed out of some material, but out of a harmonious combination of the aspects of a particular material. It is quite natural that iron will dictate one type of harmony; stone, another; and ferro-con-

1. A building should be so executed that it would not be possible within it "to make any additions or modifications without doing harm to the whole." Leone Battista Alberti, *Di* [*sic*] *re aedificatoria*.

crete, something altogether else. Instead of the false and theatrical monumentality of inert walls adorned with columns, so beloved in the nineteenth century, forms will assume a resilient and sympathetic resemblance to the inner organic life of the material.

Finally, this latter property will also give rise to a *forcefully condensed form*, one devoid of any diffuseness. Indeed, the economical utilization of a material eliminates any chance of concealing its full potential. The internal forces of the architectural organism will rise to the surface, as it were. The play of static and dynamic forces within a monument will become extremely evident.

What previously was symptomatic of artistic taste—incompleteness, fragmentation, and a certain deliberate ambiguity of form—has today, of course, assumed a different value. We require a form that is absolutely complete, distinct, and forcefully condensed. Characteristic of the preceding culture was a love of everything rendered by hand (the situation at times reached such extremes that in buildings erected in the Russian style,[a] individual parts were endowed with distorted and irregular aspects). This is explained by a real fear of anything that was well defined and made according to a precise pattern. At the present time, however, the modern architect certainly does not object to having all necessary bearing elements cast or manufactured by a mechanized process. The standardization of the production process does not intimidate us in the least. Everything that technology can provide must be accepted and organized by the architect, for his goals entail neither an unhampered search for self-contained forms nor the ambiguities produced by inspired hands, *but the clear recognition of his problems and the means and methods for their solution*. The machine can teach us about the following things as well.

Since everything in the machine is organized down to the last millimeter of its being, it follows that questions regarding the quality of a material, its treatment and surface characteristics—i.e., whether it is rough or smooth, colored or uncolored—are nearly as important as the most fundamental questions involved in any system of creativity; this naturally has aroused a heightened interest in these questions, which previously were of comparatively little concern to us. *Questions regarding the facture[b] and working of a material*, which thus are brought into sharp focus, assume tremendous importance, often becoming the paramount tools of the artist. No wonder that even painting for a certain period of time manifested such a characteristic predilection for the non-objective still life, whose only content was the sensory perception of different surfaces of wood, steel, cast iron, paper, and the like.

There can be no doubt that questions regarding the factural[c] working of the elements of form must play an exceedingly important role in the development of architecture, given that they set the conditions for craftsmanship in art; they compel the artist to leave his work studio for a more direct and intimate involvement in creating an architectural monument, with the very choice of materials and the manner of treating a wall surface or its elements representing a natural culmination of the overall orderly organization of creative work.

Thus far we have focused our attention on the purely static properties of the machine and have satisfied ourselves that the essence of the machine organism in no way conflicts with man's development of the concept of beauty, but simply propels him onto a definite and clearly expressed course for its development. Now let us turn to an examination of the machine's other properties, its dynamic features, which have enormous significance for the development of a modern aesthetic.

The concept of movement almost always assumes an invisible role in the creative intentions of the artist and always is a potential creative force, becoming rarefied in one form or another. Only through the concept of movement can the very meaning of an architectural monument, its articulation and elements, be revealed. So, precisely, in a living organism, only movement in a particular direction—the movement of the arms and legs, the rays of vision and the sound of the human voice—can delineate that organism's meaning clearly in our perceptions. By virtue of movement, we can ascertain a person's primary and secondary features and the organic meaning of the development of the human body.

In exactly the same way, apart from any utilitarian or constructive problems and apart from the architect's wishes or intentions, we can sense in every architectural monument, in its most austere design, the presence of some kind of internal dynamic system. That it is indeed possible to speak of the orderly organization of architecture even from the standpoint of external appearance is due to the presence in architectural monuments of purely rhythmical aspects which provide the key to deciphering a particular compositional method.[2] Indeed, the composi-

2. A more detailed exposition of the essence of rhythmic principles in architecture is contained in my work *Ritm v arkhitekture* [Rhythm in Architecture] (Moscow: Izd-vo "Sredi kollektsionerov," 1923).

tional essence of the most monumental and static works of architecture can only be perceived as a function of the movement of various horizontal, vertical, and, frequently, inclined forces. The concept of a static state itself simply denotes the state of equilibrium achieved by that movement as a result of the counterbalancing of opposing, mutually destructive compositional forces. This, for example, is how the art from the prime age of Hellas or

Locomotive manufactured by the Kraus factory in Munich

the art from the golden age of the Italian Renaissance can be understood. If the criteria of movement were not utilized at all in the monuments of this art, it is only because these monuments represent a self-contained world of moving forces whose resultant force not only never extends beyond the boundary of the given monument, but never even determines the direction of any movement; its resultant force in this case is simply equal to zero.

Along with the striving for such a balanced art, however, mankind has also been inclined to strive for other ideals as well—namely, for a clearer articulation of the problem of movement.

In monumental art this striving is revealed in the prevalence of horizontal forces, which primarily assume a static role in architecture. Even here, however, we are already dealing with a pronounced tendency of movement in a horizontal direction and, consequently, with a disruption of equilibrium. Still, it is vertical forces that on the whole constitute the most active source of dynamic quality; in those instances where these forces attain their greatest development, we encounter the most palpable sense of movement.

Such is the nature of Gothic art, which now is readily comprehensible as a function of an impetuous and intense striving upward. What so keenly accentuates the thrust and character of this movement is not so much the principle of vertical articulation as such, as the growing force of movement in an upward direction, which is manifested in a gradual dematerialization beginning with the piers and buttresses and ending with the tiny spires and crosses.

In precisely the same manner, the principles of dynamic forces that increase and decrease in intensity, although somewhat different in character, provide the key to deciphering the dynamic origins of the painterly[d] styles; the best example of this is the Baroque.

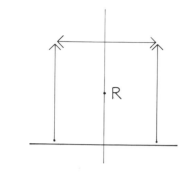

I

Movement in any Baroque monument is usually broken down into a multitude of separately articulated forces of increasing and decreasing intensity; these forces may be either diagonal (volutes; consoles; triangular, segmental, and broken pediments; and so forth), or vertical and horizontal, but the very nature of their intensification is revealed primarily by the heightened significance of their relief, modénature,[e] chiaroscuro, and so forth (the transition from a pilaster to an engaged column to a free-standing column embodying vertical forces, and the accumulated shadows cast by the cornice reliefs embodying horizontal forces).

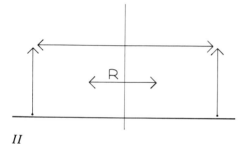

II

Yet even in this painterly art, each pair of these articulated forces achieves a counterbalance between intensification and equilibrium. Occurring within it, usually at the culminating point of its development, is an axis that either exists in fact or that can be discerned by us. In other words, a definite equilibrium, or a predisposition toward one, occurs in each pair of forces, just as it does in the pair of resultant forces integrating them. Thus, the characteristic aspect synthesizing the whole sweep of historical architecture is, for us, *that movement which is counterbalanced one way or another within the bounds of the architectural monument itself*, a movement which, even though providing for the primary development of certain forces, nonetheless allows the *establishment of their resultant force, its axis of movement always occurring within the bounds of the monument itself, for the most part within its central nucleus*. This already accounts for the essential presence of symmetrical forms at least in separate clusters if not in the overall silhouette itself.

The presence of an axis within the composition generates a composition that is balanced and symmetrical.

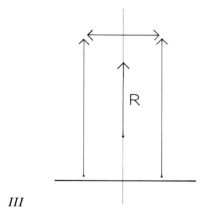

III

At this point, in order to exhaust the dynamic content of our art historical heritage, it behooves us to mention the purest source of rhythm, manifested in the square[f] or circle enclosed by porticos, and sometimes in the longitudinal development of both. Yet even these examples essentially do not deviate from the above framework. Indeed, such a square or circle has a compositional axis that occurs at the center of that square or circle, while the longitudinal movement perceivable in the portico is distingushed, as in the first example, by a *neutrality in its direction of movement*; this movement, although very clearly outlined, is essentially *neutral*. It can be viewed as easily from left to right as from right to left, clockwise as easily as counterclockwise.

Let us now turn once more to an examination of the machine. The quintessence of its being resides in movement. Any machine that is not dynamic in the most rudimentary sense of the word appears to be an obvious absurdity. The entire concept, the entire creative composition developed by its constructor, from the general plan to the minutest detail, constitutes a striving to achieve the best manifestation and embodiment of this idea of movement. To gain full command of movement, to become its actual master, to use it to cut through the hard crust of the earth and the radiant azure expanse of the atmosphere, is a problem over whose solution the creative forces of the entire world have clashed, moving successfully from one conquest to another. The machine is the source, the method, and the means of this conquest.

The motion of the machine is characterized by what for us is an extremely important feature, which stems from its basic properties. As we have already noted, the machine's orderly organization always leads to an absolutely individual solution, one which alone is capable of explaining it. Its very character is likewise the consequence of a clearly realized and precisely outlined dynamic problem. A given machine is the consequence of movement in a *particular direction* and of a particular character and purpose. What thus emerges as the distinguishing feature of the machine's dynamic properties is an actively manifested, characteristic *direction of movement*, whose modification actually leads to the destruction of the concept of the machine. The machine, in our perception, always constitutes a force that is moving or being moved in a direction that catches the eye. Thus, for example, any locomotive, motor, or locomobile[g] derives its meaning and fulfillment in relation to the direction of its movement. The very composition of the locomotive, the distribution of its individual elements—the smokestacks, wheels, furnaces, and tenders—are all functions not only of a particular movement, but also of a particular direction of this movement. For us a locomotive at rest is imbued with this same expressiveness precisely because its compositional solution is complete and conclusively establishes its dynamic purpose. In looking at a stationary locomotive, we can readily grasp its dynamic purpose, for it is conveyed by its very composition. And although movement in the opposite direction may be possible, we nonetheless perceive it as being an anomaly, an aberration of movement that violates the very meaning of the machine. Thus, a motor moving in a reverse direction not only arouses a feeling of uncertainty within us, but, according to our perception, violates its aesthetic legitimacy. Since a machine's motion is determined *entirely* by its construction, the essence of its organism, it should thus be easy for us to perceive the *axis* of that motion, that ideal line which is the object of the machine's resultant force. What assumes particular importance and significance in our perception, however, is *the fact that the axis of this motion almost always occurs outside the machine;* otherwise, it would be impossible for it to achieve its forward motion. Thus, we always perceive the ideal axis of the automobile's movement to be the purpose of that movement, to be an imaginary line that extends in front of it and always moves simultaneously with the automobile itself, representing that compositional axis around which the whole concept of the machine is constructed. In instances when the machine's motion is not an end in itself but merely a means— as, for example, in the case of the various kinds of machines with centrifugal motion—the object of the latter motion should naturally be sought in forward motion, for which centrifugal motion simply provides the means. Thus a centrifugal motor drives the belts and pulleys in a forward motion; and it is precisely to this motion that the composition of the machine is subordinated, for the object and meaning, and thus the essence of any motion in a machine, is not a self-contained motion in and of itself, but a *motion generating work in the direction of an axis located beyond that motion and representing an ideal, unrealizable objective;* for realization constitutes equilibrium, and equilibrium would nullify the active state of the machine's motion.

A machine in which the aforementioned aspects are not particularly obvious may

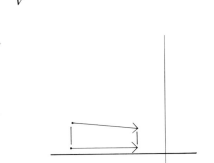

IV

V

VI

91

sometimes manifest them in the motion of some extraneous magnitudes that come into contact with the machine—that of the pulleys which glide along its length, of the material that crushes or cuts through it. This certainly does not alter the essence of the matter.

The analysis of this kind of motion in a machine reveals a new aspects of its character. Since motion occurs in the direction of an axis that lies outside the machine, with the possibility of reaching it (the axis) constituting the machine's very objective, this motion thus gives rise to a certain *unfulfillment, an unfeasible tendency,* a certain tension whose specific character is wholly at the root of the concept of the new organism. Indeed, just as the most poignant aspects of the Baroque lie in those elements which reveal an obvious unfulfillment of movement (such as, for example, broken, gouged-out cornice lines which cannot reach the axes located in their midst, or elements that are dispersed and striving to unite with their axis), so precisely all the force and poignancy embodied in the tension of purely modern organisms derive from the incompleteness and perpetual unfeasibility of dynamic tendencies, a condition keenly emphasized by the fact that the position of the axis of movement is perceived to lie either outside the general composition or within its outermost boundaries. Thus, the machine naturally gives rise to a conception of entirely new and modern organisms possessing the distinctly expressed characteristics of movement—*its tension and intensity, as well as its keenly expressed direction.* Both of these characteristics give rise to concepts of new forms, whereby the tension and concentration inherent in this movement will unwittingly—irrespective of the author's own desires—become one of the fundamental moments of artistic conception.

The other consequence resulting from the overall thrust of our discourse consists of a new definition of the machine and the new forms derived from it. An examination of movement in the architectural monuments of various historical styles indicates that the axis of movement within them always coincides with the axis of symmetry for the overall silhouette of the architectural organism; quite frequently, these monuments even represent a combination of several axes of symmetry and axes of movement. Naturally, this phenomenon cannot exist in the machine, where the axis of movement generally occurs or strives to occur beyond the machine itself. The question of symmetry in a machine is thus an altogether secondary one and not subordinated to the main compositional idea. Hence, we come to the final conclusion imposed upon us by the machine— namely, *that it is possible and natural for the modern architect's conceptions to yield a form that is asymmetrical or that, at best, has no more than a single axis of symmetry, which is subordinated to the main axis of movement and does not coincide with it.*

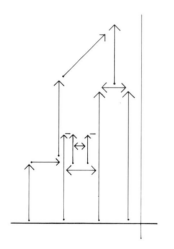

Palace of Labor by the Vesnin brothers

The diagrams accompanying this chapter convey in hypothetical and graphic terms the dynamic content of architectural organisms belonging to various stylistic groups. Figure I portrays a harmonious architecture (Greece in the fifth century B.C., Italy at the beginning of the sixteenth century) where horizontal and vertical forces are brought into complete equilibrium and where, consequently, the resultant force R of movement equals zero. Figure II represents monumental organisms (Egypt, Italy at the beginning of the fifteenth century) where horizontal forces are the predominant ones, and where the horizontal R constitutes some magnitude. Figures III and IV are schemes for organisms that are striving upward and consequently reveal a predominance of vertical forces (Gothic), while Figure IV conveys the gradual intensification of these forces along an axis of movement that coincides with symmetry. Figure V schematically depicts the system of movement in a Baroque monument; here diagonal forces, just as generally the principle of forces that increase and decrease in intensity, are revealed in a dispersal of these forces vainly striving to reach their axis of movement, which even here, however, coincides with the axis of symmetry. Finally, Figure VI represents a scheme for the movement of a machine (automobile), all of whose forces are striving for an axis of movement that lies outside of it.

The drawings appended here are of the design for the Palace of Labor by the Vesnin brothers[h] and its dynamic scheme, which represents a descriptive diagram of the modern architectural conception.

5.
Construction and Form
in Architecture.
Constructivism

*Project for the Tower of the Third
International by Tatlin*

As a result of our analysis of the machine's attributes, it is now possible to render an objective evaluation of the theory of "constructivism" being promulgated at the present time.

The actual meaning of the word is not new to us, especially as it applies to architecture, where the construction of an organism—which determines the creation of the material that isolates space and hence the character of the spatial solution—has always played a paramount role in the evolution of form.

In a vast majority of instances the true meaning of architecture is discerned primarily in its constructive aspects; the fundamental problem of architecture—delimiting the boundaries of space with material forms—requires the creation of elements that function constructively.

This is possibly how the most primitive architectural organism, the dolmen—whose object was to combine the most elementary constructive elements of post and lintel—was created. Thus, in this prehistoric architectural monument we should above all see the constructive problem.

Elevator in Buffalo

It would, however, be a serious mistake to restrict oneself to such an interpretation of architectural monuments. Along with the experience man gains from dealing with his buildings, he also develops a complex system for a self-sufficient world associated with these constructions. Modern psychophysiology has established that various elements of form (line, surface, volume), both in themselves and particularly in various juxtapositions, engender emotions of satisfaction or dissatisfaction within us, as do certain colors and sounds.[1]

Irrespective of the laws of statics or mechanics which are understood theoretically, each person develops a purely intuitive grasp of these laws, by virtue of which a vertical support that is too thin in relation to its height and load, for example, induces within us, without any reasoning or mathematical calculations, a sensation of dissatisfaction: it causes us to feel anxious and uncertain about the fitness of the architectural organism, and thereby produces a purely physiological feeling of discomfort. As a result of our perceptual experience, the mathematical laws of statics and dynamics are animated into lifelike forces of the organic world; accordingly, from the moment man takes his first steps, form exerts a spontaneous influence, which becomes increasingly more clear, distinct, and concrete.

Thus, by virtue of our brain's associative faculty, the construction of the architectural organism also acquires a somewhat different, self-sufficient significance; and, by virtue of a particular kind of association, the so-called "motor" kind, man seeks to find in this animated construction that element of movement which results in the development of form, and the reflection of which occurs during our perception of form. Lifeless forms, which affect us simply through their inert existence, take on a different life in our consciousness as fragments of universal movement, accumulating in our memory a distinct classification of the same formal images on the basis of the spatial progression of individual elements in a given arrangement. These initial motor associations are followed by others. Movement as such, the rhythm of a particular regularity manifested in architectural form, is not a neutral entity for us: it is condensed into two basic elements—the vertical and the horizontal—which enter into a certain competition or struggle.

The life of a form is imbued with what, for us, is a deeply agitating action, a true collision of two elements in the microcosm of constructive elements, reflecting two struggling elements—the boundless, static horizontality and the vigorous daring of the vertical aspect.

The constructive scheme becomes a real spectacle for us, one where the eye never ceases to follow the outcome of this struggle. Construction, as such, transcends itself; the constructive forces associated with the experiences of man's inner world create an *organic world of form*, making it a familiar and intimately understandable phenomenon; the analogy with the static and dynamic laws of the universe transforms this organic world into a world of external forms, one often equal in the energy of its impact to the powerful forces of nature. Thus, the *constructive system*, by virtue of our perceptual experience and the psychophysiological characteristics of the human being, *gives rise to yet another system, one which is self-sufficient and at the same time proceeds from and is dependent upon the construction of the world of form*—or, properly speaking, an *aesthetic* system. Moreover, in the paradigm which we have examined, both systems fully coincide. The very same element is simultaneously a utilitarian element of construction and an aesthetic element of form.

But man did not settle on this course. Once he learned to see another world besides the elements of construction, once he sensed its self-sufficient significance, he naturally wanted to develop and enrich it. Greek architecture already represents a significant elaboration of this sort. The Archaic Greek temple up until the eighth and seventh centuries B.C. was most likely built of wood, and its original system was a purely constructive one, representing the necessary combination of vertical supports, horizontal beams, and inclined braces for trussed rafters. Existing reconstructions of the wooden Doric temple provide a very plausible explanation of the origins of each of the formal elements that make up the temple's various constructive features. For us, this represents a secondary concern; what remains important is the effort of the man who has sensed the meaning and self-transcending significance of constructive forces, *whose role he began to emphasize and intensify*. As soon as the elements of construction became the elements of form, man wanted to make the life associated with construction appear to be as vivid as possible. If it were possible to resurrect the irretrievably lost wooden Doric temple before its transformation into masonry forms, we most likely would see how the static system of supports and spans was fully and emphatically revealed by the architect. We would see the actually existing constructive world, a system of internal forces *clearly and graphically interpreted*. Indeed, the very shaft of the column, growing wider toward the bottom, with vertical fluting underscoring its function, with the alignment of echinus and abacus assuming the role of a bolster, represents, as precisely as any other element of the temple, *an interpretation of its organic constructive life*.

But then the Greek architect proceeded from the wooden temple to a stone one. By this time, the *system of interpreting construction* was so firmly entrenched

1. For example, Wilhelm Wundt has determined that we experience the sensation of pleasure when we perceive a line that is more comfortable for the eye to follow—such as, for example, a vertical or horizontal line—when the muscles moving the eye have to expend a minimum of energy. By the same line of reasoning, an irregular and sharply broken line creates an uncomfortable sensation, since the eye must constantly change direction through angular movements, which cause the nerves stimulating the muscles, as well as the muscles themselves, to experience painful sensations. If crooked lines are bent with a certain degree of regularity, which provides an opportunity to prepare for anticipating the phenomenon and for its realization, they tend to produce the most profound feeling of satisfaction. In precisely the same way, regular forms are perceived more readily by the eye than irregular ones. In the realm of regular forms, a normally developed optical sense prefers forms articulated according to the simplest principles, such as symmetry or the golden section. [Wilhelm Max Wundt (1832–1920), German psychologist and physiologist, established physiological psychology as a special science that sought to employ the method of laboratory experimentation to determine the different phenomena of human consciousness and the natural correlations among them. He promulgated the concept of "psychophysiological parallelism," which held that these phenomena were inseparable from neural functions, although not causally related to them. Wundt's conception of the role of kinesthesis in perception—to which Ginzburg refers here—was outlined in his pioneering work *Grundzüge der physiologischen Psychologie* (Leipzig: W. Engelmann, 1874). This work was translated into Russian as *Osnovaniia fiziologicheskoi psikhologii*, trans. Kandinsky (2 vols.; Moscow, 1880); the latter translation was later reissued under the editorship of A. Krogius, A. Lazursky, and A. Nechaev (St. Petersburg, 1914). Among Wundt's students was the psychologist Hugo Münsterberg, whose own work on aesthetic perception at the Harvard Psychological Laboratory in 1898–1904 influenced Nikolai A. Ladovsky and others in the Rationalist movement in Soviet architecture in the 1920s.]

in the architect's mind that it became a *self-sufficient system;* and when the first stone temples began to appear, this *interpretation was transformed into a dramatization* of a non-existent life that survived in his memory by virtue of tradition. It is not at all surprising that such elements as the triglyph or capital should have become purely and solely aesthetic elements; that their organic link to construction was breached is indicated by the fact that the cuts in the stones inadvertently occurred in the middle of an element. Only in the fifth century B.C. did a moment again arise in the history of Greek architecture that can be called *organic;* construction once again overtook form, which in turn became subordinated to it.

At the same time, it is possible to discern in the Greek temple, aside from its purely constructive—i.e., constructively working—elements, other elements that were summoned into being merely by utilitarian considerations. For example, the sloping lines of the pediment constitute the constructive elements of rafter braces "working" in the temple organism, while the filling in of the pediment with a triangular wall panel constitutes simply the means, devoid of any constructive role, of achieving a more complete enclosure of the temple space. The architect acquires a capacity to distinguish one aspect from the other; naturally, as he becomes occupied with a more vivid interpretation or dramatization of the organic life of the monument, he develops a different attitude toward them.

While the architect emphasizes the constructively "working" elements in their active state, he simply decorates the "non-working" elements. The distinction between these two facets of the architect's activity is revealed most clearly in those instances when the constructive element can only be treated in a particular way, when its aesthetic organization constitutes an extremely clear-cut problem whose solution is dependent upon "givens," upon a clear understanding of them. The element that is not constructive permits significantly greater freedom; like the triangular pediment of a Greek temple, it only dictates certain limits within which the architect is free to enlist the services of the sculptor or painter. Nevertheless, in the organic period of fifth-century B.C. Greek art which we have examined, even this decorative activity was dependent upon the overall system and independent of extra-formal content, which can be anything subordinated compositionally to the general plan for organizing the temple space.

Thus, just as the dolmen showed itself to be *not only a constructive system but also an animated organic world, so the art of the fifth-century Greek temple represented not only an organic dramatization of constructively working elements, but also a subordinate system of independent "decorative" elements.*

A no less convincing example of the elusive boundary at which the "constructive" ends and the "decorative" begins is Gothic architecture, which among the numerous historical styles is essentially the most constructive. Indeed, any Gothic church represents a naked and quite unconcealed constructive system of supporting piers, vaults springing from them, and very obviously "working" flying buttresses, which are connected to supporting pylons by arched struts. This is no longer an intensification or dramatization of constructive existence, but a genuine, convincing, and rational constructive life. The feeling for the decorative, which nevertheless was sufficiently strong among Gothic artists, expressed itself in architecture, by comparison, as a highly limited sphere of activity—in the ornateness of the stained-glass window sashes, the coloration of the window panes themselves, and a few plant motifs in the capitals, gargoyles, and rose windows.

98

Nevertheless, it is extremely easy to trace through this constructive style both the vivid rhythmic system of arranging a procession of supporting pylons and the fine decorative confidence with which the forest of arched struts and gargoyles pierces the blue of the sky.

So what is this? A constructive and rational system, or the impetuous fantasy of a mystical decorator? Naturally, it is both. What we find instructive in this example is the stability of purely aesthetic perceptions, which take the content of architecture to be either a constructive system or a disinterested decorativeness, depending upon the contemporary state of life and the psychology of the artistically active social groups that are somehow involved in creating architectural monuments, or—to put it another way—depending upon the specific content of the architectural genius of the epoch.

But a second step always follows the first. Once it is acknowledged that decorative elements possess a certain independence, this independence continues to develop further. The decorative impulse, as such, once again grows beyond itself, becoming transformed into a new system for organizing surface or space. Sometimes it even ceases to be dependent upon a general architectural system, engendering its own often contrary laws. The difference between a "working" and a "non-working" element then disappears, and we can see in the development of almost every single style and frequently in wholly independent styles how form, having already become mostly decorative, enters into a contradiction with construction, reaching the level of a full-fledged conflict. At that point decorativeness as an end in itself becomes the only justification for a design, and efforts to find other objectives here would be in vain. Such, in general, was the great style of the Baroque, which gladly devoted its images to painterly problems lying totally outside the realm of constructive forces.

"Modern City." Etching by E. I. Norvert

Nevertheless, the historian cannot sustain either the justification or the condemnation of such styles. He must accept them as such; recent research on the Baroque style has shown that we are dealing here with an entity that constituted a fertile, brilliant, and, in its own way, legitimate world, one intertwined in the most tight-knit manner with all the facets of the material and spiritual culture of its time.

The constructive and decorative aspects are most frequently perceived as something mutually exclusive, as two extreme poles in the development of architectural form. However, it is exceedingly difficult to establish such a sharp distinction between them. As we have already seen, a purely constructive form possesses the capacity to grow beyond itself and to give us an utterly disinterested, i.e., aesthetic pleasure; in the same way, while decorative form has its own laws, these often merge with constructive ones. Both terms are part of a larger, more generalized aesthetic conception. An extremely simple, utilitarian, and constructive window in a wall, when a harmonious relationship among its

99

2. "We declare uncompromising war on art." First Working Group of Constructivists, 1920 [sic], Moscow. (Aleksei Gan, *Konstruktivizm* [Constructivism. Tver: Tverskoe izd-vo, 1922, p. 3].) [The date of this declaration is actually 1921, as noted correctly in Gan's book. It was in March of that year that this group of Constructivists was formed in the Institute of Artistic Culture (*Institut khudozhestvennoi kul'tury*), or INKHUK, in Moscow.]

sides and a rhythmic formula for filling up the walls with it have been developed by the architect, represents in principle the same sort of aesthetic problem as does a form exhausted by the burden of ornamentation and concealed by it; the only differences between them lie in the approaches taken by the architects in each particular instance and in these artists' creative psychology and the character of their aesthetic emotion.

Putting up a row of pillars to support a beam is a purely constructive problem; at the same time, if the architect has any thoughts about a specific rhythmic arrangement for these pillars, the problem immediately becomes a purely aesthetic one. Painting these pillars constitutes a means of protecting them from inclement weather, but as soon as the architect thinks about choosing a specific color for a color scheme, the problem immediately becomes one of decoration. Thus are all these nuances of what is essentially a single architectural sensibility intertwined in a skein, and attempts to establish their limits would be to force the issue.

In generalizing all these arguments, we should acknowledge the breadth of aesthetic emotion absorbed, for a variety of reasons, within their different aspects. Yet all of them are viable, as they are equally humane. We do not know what feelings possessed primitive man to put up his dolmen: was it a prototype for a human dwelling and a shelter from the elements, was it a manifestation of his constructive skills and their fulfillment in a purposeful application, or was it perhaps a yearning for a disinterested enjoyment of the first organization of space, the first creation of an aesthetic form? Or might it be that all these feelings motivated the prehistoric architect simultaneously?

While we are obliged from a historical standpoint to acknowledge objectively that the most diverse approaches to this problem all have an equal right to exist, we still cannot forgo a genetic examination of them.

Earlier, in the preceding chapters, we spoke of style as an independent phenomenon—of its youth, maturity, and withering away, of that distinctive language of forms and their combinations which characterizes each change in style. Having analyzed the history of styles, we shall easily to be able to discern the law that is the most characteristic of virtually every great flowering. When a new language of style emerges, when new elements of it are created, there naturally is no need to dilute them with anything else—the new comes into being for the most part as a constructive or utilitarian necessity devoid of decorative embellishments. The decorative elements that subsequently emerge do not disrupt the organic life of the monuments until such time as a surfeit of them exceeds these organic bounds, falling into a self-contained play of decorative elements. *The youth of a new style is primarily constructive, its mature period is organic, and its withering away is decorative.* Such is the model scheme for the genetic growth of a considerable number of styles. Moreover, the one exceeding all bounds—self-contained eclecticism, whose legacy remains a heavy burden for us to bear—has confirmed the genetic role of the obsolete European culture: these are the last days of its existence.

Now, from this vantage point, we shall likewise attempt to evaluate modern "constructivism" as an artistic phenomenon. Perhaps now we shall be better able to comprehend both the menacing slogan advanced by the Russian Constructivists[2] and its bravado, which are quite natural psychologically and quite familiar to the art historian: there has never, it seems, been a young movement

100

which feeling its power, did not wish in its own time and place to press for the abolition of everything that did not conform to its precepts. Furthermore, the emergence at this time of a tendency such as Constructivism not only in Russia but also in Europe (where in most instances, however, it does not seek even verbally to abolish art but regards itself as representing its modern manifestation) is all the more natural precisely because it marks a new stage in the evolution of a cycle of new artistic ideas. Never have we sensed as we do now the purely historical termination of the forms of classical art, which we have continued to live off of through inertia in recent times; never have we sensed so clearly that the fine and living creation which recently surfaced among us is merely a wax mannequin, a perfect exhibit, whose rightful place is in the museum.

Undoubtedly the course of history has come full circle. The old cycles have been completed, we are now beginning to cultivate a new field of art, and, as always happens in such instances, the problems associated with utilitarian and constructive aspects are regarded to be of paramount importance; the new style is aesthetically simple and organically logical.

This is why the ideas of Constructivism, for all their destructive promises, appear to us at the present moment to be natural, necessary, and vivifying.

If such a "constructivism" is generally characteristic of any primordial conditions for a new style, it should prove especially characteristic of the style of our times. The reason for this, of course, must be sought not only in the economic circumstances of modernity, but also in the extraordinary psychological role which has begun to be assumed in our lives by the machine and the mechanized life associated with it, whose essence consists of the bare constructive aspects of its component organisms.

In the machine there are no elements that are "disinterested" from the standpoint of elemental aesthetics. There are no so-called "free flights of fancy." Everything in it has a definite and clear-cut constructive task. One part provides support, another rotates, a third produces forward motion, and a fourth transfers that motion to the pulleys.

That is why the machine with the most actively functioning parts, with an absolute lack of "non-working" organs, quite naturally leads to an utter disregard of decorative elements, for which there is no more room, leads precisely to the idea of Constructivism, so prevalent in our time, which must by its very being absorb the "decorative," its antithesis.

The point is not, as some Constructivists are trying to persuade us, that aesthetic emotion has disappeared; that, fortunately, is not the case, and this is best proved by the work of the Constructivists themselves; rather, the point is that under the influence of the transformed conditions of life and the significance of modern economics, technology, and the machine and its logical consequences, *our aesthetic emotion, its character, has been transformed as well.* There remains and always will remain within us a need for the aesthetically disinterested, since this constitutes one of the fundamental and unshakable characteristics of our physical or, if you will, biological nature, but the satisfaction of that need is at present taking a different course. *The most desirable decorative element for us is precisely the one which is unvarnished in its constructive aspect; thus, the concept of the "constructive" has absorbed within itself the concept of the "decorative,"* has merged with it and caused this entanglement of concepts.

101

The capacity for aesthetic perception as such exists within us all, and the element best satisfying that perception at the present time is constructive form in its naked, unvarnished aspect. Hence, our reconciliation to the landscape of the new life, hence the paintings by artists and the models by stage directors that willingly treat particular elements of construction, the machine, and engineering structures as decorative motifs.

Undoubtedly there is nothing accidental in modern art's striving for an austere and ascetic language of constructive forms, just as there is nothing accidental about the epithets that the various artistic groups willingly assign themselves. "Rationalism,"[a] "Constructivism," and all such nicknames are only outward representations of a striving for modernity, one which is more profound and fertile than might seem the case at first glance and which is engendered by the new aesthetic of a mechanized life.

It is worth casting a glance at the works of architects and painters, stage directors and other masters—those who are fiercely proclaiming the death of art—as well as at the works of those who have not yet been able to bring themselves to leave the eclecticism and pseudo-romanticism of recent decades completely behind them; we can see in both categories, depending upon the degree of the artist's sensitivity and talent, the same striving for an art that is logical and rational, simple and sober—much more an art of handicraft than an art of enthusiastic inspiration, much more a profoundly straightforward and advertising art than a listlessly sentimental and rarefied one. Constructivism, as one of the facets of a modern aesthetic, born of clamorous life, steeped in the odors of the street, its maddening tempo, its practicality and everyday concerns, and its aesthetic, willingly absorbing within itself the "Palace of Labor" and the advertising posters for popular festivals, is unquestionably one of the characteristic aspects of the new style, avidly accepting modernity in all its positive and negative aspects.

6.
Industrial and Engineering
Organisms

*Interior of one of the buildings at the
Ansaldo airplane factory in Turin*

Will the machine really replace art? Will art really abandon all its artistic principles and merely imitate this audacious offspring of human invention?

Of course not. For necessity in art, in the creation and consumption of artistic treasures, probably constitutes one of the innermost foundations of human nature, the best means of heightening the intensity of human life and its social and organizational energy, pertaining in equal measure to the savage and child and to the ultramodern mechanized person. This is so also because a genuine art never consists in imitation, never abandons its organizational heights, but represents a self-contained world of laws and principles that are just adequate for life. Yet this very adequacy already forces art to be modern; for, to repeat Wölfflin's words, "forms of art say the same thing in their own language as do the voices that are contemporary to it."[1]

Thus, the above analysis of the machine as a factor playing such a powerful role in modernity and sharply transforming both our psychology and our world outlook has meaning only as a means of clarifying those aspects of modernity that can be particularly useful in the still difficult matter of prognosticating modern forms. The fundamental principles we have deduced from the essence of the machine itself are already becoming general principles, interpreting, in a certain sense, the various kinds of human activity and modernity itself. The machine, which man summoned into being and adapted to himself, is likewise adapting man, his psychology, to itself. The man flying through the air and rushing underground, turning night into day, and with his orderly organization achieving what was hitherto impermissible is a modern man; and given his practical and sober philosophy of modernity, he cannot, of course, be satisfied with grandmotherly idylls. Whether we like or dislike this man and this modernity is a question of

Bridge at the station in Cologne-on-the-Rhine

taste and, in the present instance, a rather idle question at that. Life simply is the way it is because it cannot be any other way; and just as it seems pointless to us to lament the loss of the poetry of the past and the feeble attempts to restore it, so it is important and essential to grasp the life that surrounds us and to begin creating a modern life that, if not for us then for the younger generation, will be the only poetry that it will properly comprehend. To sense the signification of the resounding ensemble of modern life; to become steeped in its concerns and joys, its landscape, its skies pierced with wires and soaring planes; to comprehend the distances that have been dwarfed by the machine's movement, the streets cut through by the sharp silhouette of the bridge and the intensely glittering specks of passers-by among them—to feel all this and to formulate it in an adequate expression is the task of modern art.

But how can we bridge the gap between this entire ensemble of modernity and the architectural monument when we realize perfectly well that the only analogy possible here lies in the principles of creative work and not in the forms themselves? We shall endeavor to continue with our analysis.

The immediate consequences of the machine, its logical development, are the so-called engineering structures that have grown out of the same modern needs of mankind. A number of similar structures are direct descendants of the machine. Such, for example, is the winch or crane, which in its compositional principles fully duplicates the machine, but in its formal elements is a typical engineering structure. Indeed, the literal meaning of the crane resides in a movement that produces a certain kind of work. Its entire organism represents a scheme that is already well known to us, one that is particular and precise in its organization, with a clearly expressed axis of movement lying outside the boundaries of the crane's organism. This essentially is the very same machine, with its characteristic intensity of movement. Nevertheless, in its outward appearance it is something else: a girder made up of bars and diagonal struts, with compressive and tensile stresses accumulating from joint to joint all the way to the top, radiating this ladder of stresses into the active work of the crane. While the organism of the machine is massive and solid, intended for movement along the ground, the structure of the crane is light, as though devised to fill the urban skyline with its well-proportioned silhouette. In the context of exterior design, this is a totally new and different organism in comparison to the machine, though one still capable, on the strength of their similar compositional principles, of combining easily with the machine in one resounding ensemble. They are adequate to one another and, placed side by side, comprise, for all their dissimilarities, a single whole.

The next level of engineering structures, one still more remote from the machine, consists of various kinds of bridge girders that involve no actual or realizable movement whatever; nevertheless, the nakedness of their structure, consisting of the now familiar, intense stresses of bars and joints connecting them, represents an extremely vivid and distinct scheme for the movement being transferred from one embankment to another. Here as in the crane, the new organism, compared to the machine, serves a different purpose, is made of different materials, and is designed differently.

The direct connection between such an iron girder and the stone material of the bridge abutment quite naturally continues the same line of development, seeking an adequate form in stone. Indeed, the monumental and monolithic abutment is built according to the very same principle; it clearly manifests the stresses of intensive work being performed in a certain direction and associated with all the stresses in the bars of the girder: the silhouette of the masonry abutment represents a truly modern element of form. Thus, we see how different problems that are encompassed by a single common principle do not at all result in their repetition and identical design; rather they create elements of form which are different and self-sufficient, but which nonetheless say one and the same thing in different languages. Thus, the method for seeking new forms and the role of the modern machine aesthetic as a primary source of that method are indicated to a certain extent by an examination of modern engineering structures.

However, the gulf is still too great between the formal elements of the latter and purely architectural forms. Neither the machine nor the engineering structure provides us with an expressive *spatial* solution, one which constitutes a true manifestation of architecture. Our assimilation of this method will be made somewhat easier by an analysis of another kind of structure, which also emanates directly from the machine but which already bears a greater affinity to what in everyday life is, in a strict sense, termed "architecture"—namely, industrial structures. The factory is the most natural consequence of the development of the machine. It unites within itself a whole assembly of machines, which are sometimes homogeneous, sometimes heterogeneous, but always bound together by one and the same common purpose. Such an assembly of machines is

1. [Ginzburg does not cite the source for this quote. The basic idea, though not the exact wording here, is expressed by Wölfflin in *Kunstgeschichtliche Grundbegriffe* (1915), translated into Russian as *Istolkovanie iskusstva*, trans. and intro. by B. Vipper (Moscow: Del'fin, 1922). Discussing the way in which styles express their epoch, he writes, "It is obviously a new ideal of life which speaks to us from Italian Baroque, and although we have placed architecture first as being the most express embodiment of that ideal, the contemporary painters and sculptors say the same thing in their own language . . ."; *Principles of Art History*, trans. M. D. Hottinger (New York: Dover, 1950), p. 10.]

imbued by a movement that is infinitely more intense than that of each individual machine; at the same time, the heterogeneous machines that are united by one common purpose are an example of an even more striking and orderly compositional organization. If we have before us an assembly of machines serving a single mode of production—say, for example, one for manufacturing matches—where one machine processes the shavings, another one transforms them into a box, a third produces the matches, a fourth dips them in sulfur, and so on, then all these machines are bound together by the same iron necessity that binds the elements of the individual machine to one another. Indeed, the placement of these machines, the direction of their axes, the incline of the different elements—all this is strictly organized and, in addition, materially united by the belts of pulleys and gears. And given that the production process begins at one end of the assembly and terminates at the opposite end, we have a sharply emphasized direction of movement here. On the other hand, the assemblage in one place of a multitude of machines bound by one and the same purpose creates a fresh new feeling of power by virtue of the increasing force of these organized stresses. The endless number of steel monsters hissing and roaring, interlaced by the sliding belt lines moving intensely and incessantly in a single direction—all this gives rise to a previously unknown tension of monumental movement.

Elevator in Buffalo

The factory envelops this monumental movement, representing a grandiose envelope for it, and must certainly express all of its characteristic aspects. On the other hand, it already represents a kind of housing—true, a housing more for labor and machines than for man, but housing nevertheless—i.e., a veritable work of architecture, with all its spatial characteristics; hence, an analysis of such industrial structures should be of great importance to us.

In reality, of course, we can only see the basic aspects of the machine's compositional principles in any engineering structure, in any factory, elevator, or electrical plant, in those cases where the creator of these structures was steeped in their very spirit, responding with the most concise and economical means to the utilitarian and constructive problems given him. And quite naturally, constructors and engineers on their own, without any deliberate intention, perhaps without the involvement of any architects at all, created those monuments of modern form which, in the realm of an already realized architecture, of structures that have already been built, are virtually the only ones with the right to be defined as such. Indeed, in all of them we can analyze familiar characteristics: both a genuine monumentality and a purely modern dynamism of that monumentality; an asymmetry of form; a sharply expressed direction of movement, growing in the direction of a clearly perceived external axis and creating the characteristic pathos of a mechanized town; the strength and indestructibility of the compositional scheme, cohesive despite its seeming randomness; the laconism and distinct economy of all the individual elements and articulations; and finally, the particularly rich and crisp textures of materials, as evidenced in the interplay of iron and steel, with their expressively silhouetted dynamic aspects, the taut solidity of stone and ferro-concrete, and the reflective glitter of glass, coalescing all these aspects into a whole. In the industrial structures of the last decade in the largest cities of Europe and America we see already realized not only the foundations of a modern aesthetic, but even individual elements of architecture, systems of supports, joints, spans, openings, terminations, flashes of compositional schemes and flashes of new form, which can already be transferred to domestic architecture, can already serve as the concrete and profoundly practical material that will be able to help the architect find a true course for creative work and help transform the language of abstract aesthetics into a precise lexicon of architecture. Such is the role of industrial architecture: the role of a connecting link whose principal value for us consists in its prosaic earnestness, everyday reality, rooting of creative pursuits in the firm ground of the present day, and its keeping high-flown daydreams within the limits of what is possible, attainable, and truly necessary.

Thus, should the forms of industrial architecture not supplant all other forms of architectural creativity? Should factories and silos be the only content of modern architecture?

Of course not. Just as we established the interdependence between the machine and industrial structures, so must an analogous interdependence be established between industrial structures and the architecture of the residential building. Just as industrial architecture is not a conscious imitation of the machine and its forms are merely adequate for the purpose, created organically and quite independently but nonetheless reflecting with all their characteristic originality the very same modernity, so precisely a similar analogy is applicable here. And if in the preceding century when the basic meaning of life was different the main content of architecture lay in the residential building and the public building, which influenced industrial architecture, then at present precisely the reverse phenomenon is taking place: industrial architecture, standing closer to the sources of a modern understanding of form, must exert an influence on domestic architecture, which is the most traditional and stagnant of all.

It is from industrial architecture rather than from anywhere else that we can expect realistic indications concerning how and in what way these paths can be found. What we are talking about here is adding to the existing landscape of modernity—the machine, the engineering and industrial structures—the latest link in the architectural chain: residential and public buildings equal to these structures.

7.
The Characteristic Aspects of the New Style

4500 cbm.st.

35 m hoch

Steam coolers at the Tissen machine factory

W hat, then, are the roads that lie immediately ahead for the creator of the residential and public building?

Is it possible to speak of a formal language for these branches of architectural creativity?

Certainly this question cannot as yet receive a definitive answer. The events that shook the world at large and by their significance facilitated the revelation and explanation of the basic artistic problems of modernity have their contrary side as well.

The economic depression holding virtually all the countries of the world in its grip has hardly allowed any of them to produce a brilliant picture of housing construction. The large architectural structures put up in the past decade barely number in the tens. In the majority of instances, only industrial structures are being erected. The reconstruction of those parts of Europe devastated by the war is proceeding under the watchword of the greatest possible reduction of pressing building programs. Naturally, all this has even greater applicability in economically more ravaged Russia.

Elevator in Buffalo

Thus, there simply does not yet exist a sufficient quantity of erected buildings or an altogether concrete body of material to provide the basis for arriving at any final conclusions about, or assessing the virtues and shortcomings of, the new style. Its outward aspect has not yet been fully developed; this will be possible only when the improvement of the country's general well-being and accumulation of wealth make it feasible to realize the best ideals of modern architecture. This will be the apogee, the blossoming of the new art.

For the time being, we can speak only of a *transitional epoch*, of a primordial stage in the development of the new style, *of those of its characteristics which have already been rather clearly determined*, but which, it goes without saying, do not exhaust all further development of the style.

The aforementioned economic pressures are already affecting this transitional epoch, forcing their mark on the already developed characteristics of the new style. Unrestrained creative fantasies, the manipulation of self-contained creative devices, are not appropriate for us at present. The conditions in which our style is now developing cannot support an extravagant and "aimless" art, for which there is no place in a modern life preoccupied and weighed down with many burdens. It is perfectly natural that life, such as it is, disciplines the artist, holding him within the limits of what is reasonable and expedient. If there can emerge in our times the notion of the death of art, one assuming nothing but "disinterested" emotions of an aesthetic nature, then it is also natural that the architect should give serious thought, first and foremost, to exploiting his "interested" potentials, i.e., to extracting all the potentially creative material languishing in the everyday utilitarian problems that he is solving. Let us not be

112

dismayed by the narrow scope of this problem. The genuine architect is too well aware of the grand picture of creation that can emerge from this small and limited source. Moreover, the thoughtful architectural historian is equally well aware of the fact that this limited purpose was the dominant thread, the genuine source, for numerous and significant architectural styles.

Thus, the economic characteristics of our transitional period are narrowing and focusing the architect's attention, first of all, on *using and organizing everyday utilitarian material* with the most concise expressiveness, with the least expenditure of human energy. In other words, they compel the careful weighing and evaluating not only of the task posed by life itself, but also of the means for its realization. They compel the architect to *construct* his problem, they compel him to exploit all the qualities and potentialities of building materials and the best, most perfected constructions of the present day.

Thus, the architect must take yet another step from his dizzying isolation down to actual reality; he must also learn from the constructor, closely scrutinizing his work. And perhaps in doing so he may be consoled by the realization that up until the eighteenth century there was no difference whatever between these two realms of activity, that the architect and the engineer were in essence synonyms of one and the same idea, and that even for the architect of the late Renaissance, the construction of any kind of engineering structure was simply part of his work.

The elimination of boundaries between the architectural significance of the factory and of the residential building, essentially but variations on the architectural problem, and the amicable rapprochement in practical work between the constructor-engineer and the organizer-architect will open up a whole series of brilliant opportunities. Then the bane of our time, whereby the constructor creates his system without believing in its absolute aesthetic cogency and expects the architect and decorator to complete it, will disappear, and the artists and architects will cease creating their often useless and contrived "constructions."

The modern state of technical science, which is making steady and rapid progress, will in the course of its dynamic life have to attract the hitherto stagnant architecture as well. The new organisms of the industrial and engineering structures, being more sensitive and closer to the noises of life, will also have to pour new juices into other organisms—into architectural monuments, imbuing them with an authentically modern character, helping to develop a *new system for the architectural organization of space.*

The shaping of modern man's new way of life will provide the point of departure for these pursuits, for which the paradigms will be industrial and engineering structures—the leading outposts of modern form.

Yet at the same time, such restrictions of the architect's creative efforts must yield other results as well. In dealing with the prosaic aspects of life, in drawing closer to the master craftsman and the constructor, the architect must unavoidably become infected by their *method of work*. He, like they, will set as his goal not the unrestrained fantasy of a detached scheme, but the clear solution of a problem into which are factored certain givens and certain unknowns. The architect will then feel himself to be *not a decorator of life, but its organizer*. Creative fantasy, the liberated energy of the spirit, will not abandon his creativity,

113

but will only be channeled in another direction. Fantasy will turn into inventiveness, life will transform it not into a plaything of leisure, but into the world that constantly surrounds us. We are well aware of the apprehensions that are common in such instances among those who overrate the "mysteriousness" of the creative process, who anticipate losing this "mystery" and, with it, the value of creativity itself. However, it is well not to confuse concepts. As no manifestation of genius in formal expression can ever be fully explained, and as we know of no conclusive answer to these questions, there exists a certain degree of insolubility about the creative process, which guarantees us both variety in individuality and the importance of our own perceptions. But this same "degree of insolubility" also exists in the creativity of the inventor, whose lot is that of one who is mysteriously chosen; the characteristic aspects of his specific course likewise cannot fully be explained. Nevertheless, the inventor knows precisely what he is striving for, solves the problems that stand before him, and this constitutes one of the tokens of his success.

Nor should it be feared that the artist will lose something of his creativity as a result of clearly knowing what he wants, what he is striving for, and what gives meaning to his work. Hence, subconscious and impulsive creativity will have to be replaced by a *clear and distinct organizational method* that economizes the architect's creative energy and transfers its liberated surplus into the inventiveness and power of the creative impulse.

Fiat automobile factory in Turin

Under the influence of this method there has likewise emerged the characteristic phenomenon of our time— *the overcoming and transformation of the old classical system of architectural thought*.

The first steps in this transformation began with the stripping of the classical architectural organism of all the varied richness of its artistic and historical accessories. The most varied capitals, columns, consoles, and corbels; the most complex molding[a] of cornices; and the whole treasure trove of decorative elements—all this unlimited heritage, which had meaning and significance only in its own time, when each detail had flowed logically out of an integral whole—all this has been dropped from the modern architect's repertory. Virtually all of us have learned to make do without this baggage, have felt ourselves estranged from this most superficial and striking manifestation of the past.

Thus the first step was taken, and it inevitably involved additional ones as well, which led in earnest to new tasks.

Architectural monuments laid bare and cleansed of their glittering and superficial attire appeared with all the fascination and unexpected sharpness of an artistic asceticism, with all the power of a rough and austere language of simple, uncluttered architectural forms.

Thus, even this first step revealed not only the overcoming of the old, but also *the specific inclination of the new toward a simple and clear expression*, the causes of which we have already sufficiently explained. Yet this cleansing of the elements of architectural form also possesses another significance, one even

114

more fraught with consequences. Since the column and the pilaster in the new architecture lose their self-contained decorative significance and remain only as constructive and utilitarian supports and buttresses, clear in their actual function, there arises before the architect in all its purity the *problem of the rhythmic organization of these supports or buttresses*. And in precisely the same way, utilitarian elements such as window or door openings, freed of their decorative garb, will compel the architect to turn to the more substantive and fundamental problem of finding *the proportional relationships, the harmonious formulas, which were lost in the labyrinth of historical accessories*.

Once a site has been cleared, all its characteristic aspects become more evident. And just as the simplification of architectural elements facilitates their more effective organization, so precisely the loss of the self-contained role that the *wall surface* had previously assumed leads the architect to a clear understanding of his most important and profound task. The wall surface and its rhythmic articulation, the proportional interdependence of all elements—all this finds its primary purpose in *the problem of enveloping space, creating its boundaries, organizing it according to definite principles*.

The legacy of the old classical system does not at this point appear hopelessly bankrupt. It gives us a guiding theme for further work. Yet it also convinces us of the complexity and significance that the spatial problem has attained in present-day architecture. What emerges as our legacy is neither any one epoch nor any one style, but the quintessence of the whole of mankind's architectural past. We feel equally *close to the purposeful clarity of the spatial solutions of the Greco-Italic system and to the desire to exploit the latent dynamic forces revealed in the tension of the Gothic and Baroque.*

Testing track on the roof of the Fiat automobile factory in Turin

And yet in spite of the completeness of both attributes in the forms of past epochs, their applications at the present time strike us as being both ineffectual and inexpressive. *The scale and force of these now-resurrected attributes are being developed to an incredible extent.*

Certainly the complexity of modern architectural organisms, multifaceted in breadth and height, is very far removed from the clear and unified cella of the Hellenic temple, from the now seemingly too simple and placid Renaissance palaces. To bring a purposeful clarity and an expressive rationality to the housing of our time, which consists of hundreds upon hundreds of units; which has no predilection for longitudinal, latitudinal, or centralized development; which emerges only under the pressure of the multitude of varied and concrete conditions of urban construction; and which for the most part is constrained to develop in a vertical direction—upward—all this compels the architect to be armed from head to toe, to be not just the chosen one endowed with the mark of genius, but also to master to perfection all the methods of architectural creativity.

On the other hand, the dynamics of the Gothic or the Baroque cathedral seem to us to be infinitely balanced and ingenuous in comparison with the irrepressible tempo of our time.

115

This compels the architect to examine carefully all the manifestations of the dynamic life of modernity in order to condense it in works of architecture with all the power and incisiveness at his disposal. Neither the means of the Gothic nor the tools of the Baroque are any longer suitable. Having discovered and mastered their compositional methods, the modern architect must continually augment them—in other words, supplement them with his own methods and his own resources, reinforced by the life that surrounds us.

Thus, each of the principles of our classical heritage must be modified at least *quantitatively* in order to prove useful for the present day. But this quantitative modification actually constitutes architecture's *new qualities* as well, for it consists in replacing outdated methods with new ones, combining still-valid methods with those that have newly been invented.

However, what further modifies our attitude toward the heritage of the past is the *synthesis* of it. In historical examples of architecture, the North and the South were always opposed to one another. The dynamics and pathos of the northern Gothic style were always directed toward the destruction and diminution of the clarity and precision of the Greco-Italic scheme.

The modern architect is destined to overcome this contradiction, to create its resounding and harmonious synthesis.

Elevators in Buffalo

Indeed, now that the new conditions of life and rapid channels of communication are narrowing the difference between the North and the South, and the successes of technology and the achievements of modern culture are equalizing the general level of European accomplishments, this contradiction is naturally bound to disappear, not through an obliteration of the particularities of their combined characteristics, but through a continual augmentation of their power by their mutual interpenetration. Purposeful clarity and unity of conception in modern architecture can attain their brilliant realization only by means of the most dynamic energizing of the monument, by means of utilizing the all-encompassing forces of tension that permeate an architectural work from entrance step to crowning pinnacle. On the other hand, the dynamic sources of architecture must not be aimed at an obliteration of the clarity of conception, but must obtain new strength and incisiveness, accentuated by the clarity of organizational method.

That there is nothing paradoxical in these words is something of which we are easily convinced by an analysis of modern industrial structures, which already show signs of this creative synthesis, containing perhaps a grain of the historical predetermination of the new style, its ties of continuity with the past, and, simultaneously, its independent force of days to come.

Yet it certainly would be extremely one-sided to suppose that this synthesis represents the only historical mission of the new style. From this melting pot we shall also have to draw a good deal that is as yet impossible to foresee, for which it is as yet impossible to find a definition. However, it is too early to be speaking about all this.

At the same time, rationalism and the conditions of modern technology are clarifying another characteristic of the new style, one that is fraught with consequences. What we are talking about is the *standardization of building production,* the mechanized mass production of individual architectural details, of individual component parts.

In its innermost essence, this principle is something that has been inherent in architectural creativity from the first stages of its existence.

When the Egyptian architect came upon the idea of making dried bricks of identical size, thereby greatly facilitating the art of building, he was acting on the strength of an economic process that dictated man's need to economize the energy he expended in every possible way. Yet such a prosaic reason not only did not impede, but actually gave rise to the emergence of a modular system which impelled man toward an organizational method in which all the parts of a composition assumed a proportional relationship to the system's module, in this instance the brick dimensions. This seemingly insignificant reason constitutes, in essence, the fundamental point of the harmonious creativity that stands out in the golden age of Hellenic architecture or in the architecture of the Italian Renaissance.

But was it not the initial standardization of production—the production of identical bricks—that proved the source of the modular system in general?

On the other hand, the jealous guardians of the magical mystery of past perfections assume an anxious and worried look at the very mention of modern standardization.

And yet surely the architecture of the great and authentic styles of the past speaks to us most tellingly of the fact that there is no such thing as a technical achievement that cannot benefit the art of architecture.

There is, of course, a difference between standardization in Egyptian architecture and standardization in our own time, between small dried bricks and the factory-cast whole blocks of architecture, individual supports, and, finally, individual housing units, which modern production can manufacture more rapidly than was possible with the Egyptian brick.

Certainly there is a difference, and this difference constitutes the evolutionary advantage of modernity, its accomplishments—that quantitative difference which must become one of the attributes of the new style. If the small dried Egyptian brick could lead to the scale of the pyramids, then what is the scale that the architect must define for himself under the conditions of modern standardization?

This scale is likewise clear. It is a scale of astounding sweep, a scale of grandiose ensembles, whole urban complexes; it is the scale of a problem that is arising before us for the first time in all its magnitude—the scale of *town planning* in its broadest scope.

However, even when applied to more modest problems, this conception will be a multifaceted and creative one, in which standardization must not only engender its own modular system for the new style, but perhaps also serve as a source for the emergence of as yet untried means.

The new style must change the whole aspect of life, must not only seek out solutions to the spatial problem in interior architecture, in its interiors, but also extend them to the exterior as well, treating volumetric architectural masses as a

117

means to the spatial solution of the city as a whole.

Certainly this will not be the idyllic garden city of the recent past, the enthusiasm for which was so greatly overdone, but a gigantic new world in which not a single achievement of the modern genius will fail to be used or drawn into the creative mainstream.

But where is the "poetry and romance" of life to be found in this mechanized hell? the frightened reader will ask.

In the very same place, of course. In the sounds and noises of the new town, in the rush of the boisterous streets, and in the characteristics of the new style, firmly welded to modern life and clearly reflected in monumentally dynamic works of architecture.

Poetry and romantic feelings should not be sought out in places where sweet-smelling hothouse flowers grow. "Poetic" material, as such, simply does not exist.

There are no reasons to worry that the powerful and constructive language of the forthcoming architecture will mean the death of man's blissfully "disinterested" perceptions.

If life should require it, poets too will be found to sing the praises of this new world; however, just as the content of this poetry will be changed, so too the language of these songs will be modified, becoming as clear and assured as the movement of the machine, as the whole life surrounding it, saturated with the juices of its time.

Illustrations.
Reflections of the New Style in the Works of Modern Russian Architects

The illustrations included in the present book are not directly related to the text, whose only aim has been to focus attention on the theoretical problem of elucidating the fundamental causes of the rise of the modern style and its conditions for growth.

The author consciously resisted the tempting opportunity afforded by the illustrative material to venture into a formal analysis and criticism of it. This is primarily because he considers this effort to be somewhat premature in the realm of theoretical analysis: the scope of the subject matter taken up by our modern architects is too limited; the number of already erected buildings is too insignificant.

Nevertheless, given that these pages are not so much the fruits of abstract thinking as the discourses of an architect who has given thought to the modernity that surrounds him, the author could not quite suppress the desire to illustrate his ideas with architectural material that, while perhaps still incomplete, is nonetheless already sufficiently revealing even in that state.

In selecting the material, the author endeavored to be as objective as possible and to represent the various groupings of architects whose work reveals, to a greater or lesser degree, a feeling for the new forms, and consequently might have some genetic significance in the formation of the new style.

In this sense, a thoughtful and impartial glance should discern a striving for pared-down, constructively accentuated forms in the essentially classical architecture of I.V. Zholtovsky— even in the whimsy of the overt window dressing of his Triumphal Arch— as well as in the artistic asceticism and

Elevator in Buffalo

rational inventiveness of the foremost disciples of Constructivism, despite the vast gulf separating their respective ideologies and formal vocabularies. And in precisely the same way the author deemed it desirable to illuminate, even if to a limited extent, not only projects for a large and monumentally scaled architecture, but also an architecture of small objects, given that the imprint of a style can and should be found in large and small objects alike.

Purely technical circumstances made it necessary, regrettably, to limit the reproductions included here only to those of Russian architects.

Nevertheless, the author expresses the hope that the appended illustrative material as a whole—neither divided up according to hostile camps nor labeled with the attendant nicknames for which we now have such a penchant—will prove sufficiently meaningful and help concretize his theoretical discourses.

Thus, a significant share of the work has been shifted onto the shoulders of those architects who kindly made their works available for the above-mentioned purpose, for which the author extends them his deepest gratitude.

*1 I. V. Zholtovsky, with N. Ia. Kolli and
V. D. Kokorin. Pavilion of the Cultural
and Educational Department at the
Agricultural Exhibition in Moscow.*

2 *I. V. Zholtovsky, with N. Ia. Kolli and M. P. Parusnikov. Auditorium at the Agricultural Exhibition in Moscow.*

3 I. V. Zholtovsky, with N. Ia. Kolli, V.
D. Kokorin, A. L. Poliakov, and M. P.
Parusnikov. Interior court of the
Machine-Building Pavilion at the
Agricultural Exhibition in Moscow.

4 *I. V. Zholtovsky, with P. A. Golosov,*
N. Ia. Kolli, V. D. Kokorin, and S. E.
Chernyshev. Manege for the Animal
Husbandry Department at the
Agricultural Exhibition in Moscow.
5 *I. V. Zholtovsky, with I. I. Nivinsky.*
Triumphal Arch at the Agricultural
Exhibition in Moscow.

6 V. A. Shchuko. Cafe for the Foreign
Department at the Agricultural
Exhibition in Moscow.

*7 V. A. Shchuko. Foreign Department at
the Agricultural Exhibition in Moscow.
Mural by A. A. Extor.*

8 E. I. Norvert. New boiler room for an electrical power station outside Moscow.

*9 E. I. Norvert. New boiler room for an
electrical power station outside Moscow.*

10 E. I. Norvert. Liapinsky Electrical
Station in Yaroslavl.

11 E. I. Norvert. Trestle for the Liapinsky
Electrical Station in Yaroslavl.

12 L. A., A. A., and V. A. Vesnin.
Project for the Palace of Labor.

13 L. A., A. A., and V. A. Vesnin.
Project for the Palace of Labor.

*14 L. A., A. A., and V. A. Vesnin.
Project for the Arcos Joint-Stock
Company Building.*

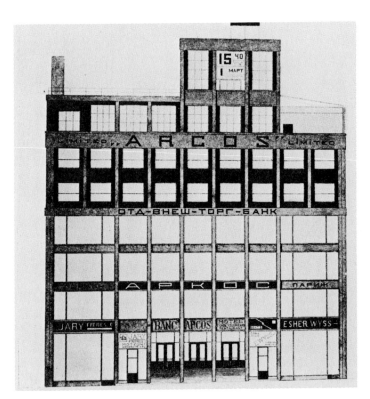 

15 L. A., A. A., and V. A. Vesnin.
Project for the Arcos Joint-Stock
Company Building.
16 L. A., A. A., and V. A. Vesnin.
Project for the Arcos Joint-Stock
Company Building.

17 A. A. Vesnin. Model of the stage set for
The Man Who Was Thursday *at the*
Moscow Kamernyi [Chamber] Theater.

18 K. S. Melnikov. "Makhorka" Pavilion
at the Agricultural Exhibition in
Moscow.
19 K. S. Melnikov. "Makhorka" Pavilion
at the Agricultural Exhibition in
Moscow.

20 I. A. Golosov. Project for the Palace of
Labor.
21 I. A. Golosov. Project for the Palace of
Labor.

*22 I. A. Golosov. Project for the Ostankino
Horse-Breeding Farm.*

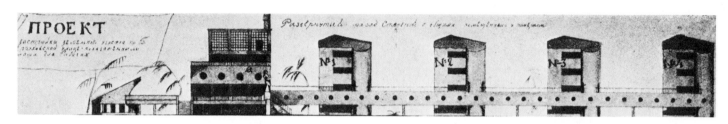

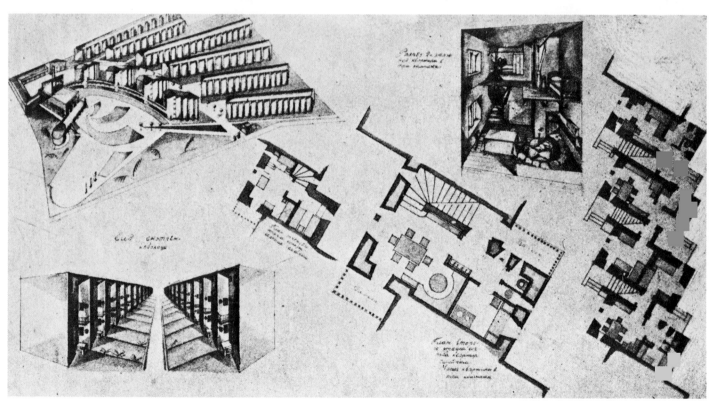

23 *K. S. Melnikov. Project for model*
workers' houses.

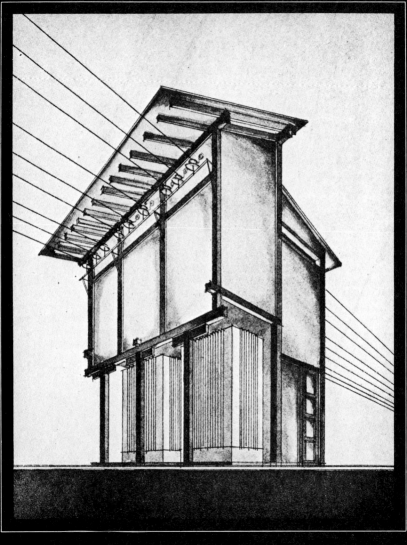

24 N. Ia. Kolli. Project for a transformer

25 M. Ia. Ginzburg and A. Z. Grinberg.
Project for the Palace of Labor.
26 M. Ia. Ginzburg and A. Z. Grinberg.
Project for the Palace of Labor.

27 M. Ia. Ginzburg and A. Z. Grinberg.
Project for the Palace of Labor.

*28 M. Ia. Ginzburg and N. A. Kopeliovich.
Model of the Lokshin House in
Eupatoria.*

29 M. Ia. Ginzburg and N. A. Kopeliovich.
Model of the Lokshin House in
Eupatoria.

30 G. M. Liudvig. Project for the Palace
of Labor.

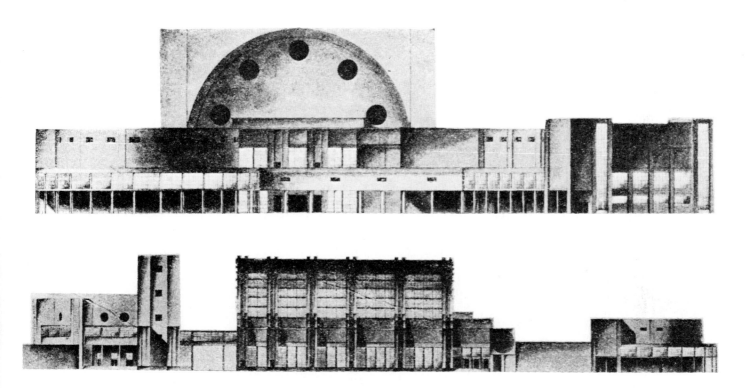

*31 M. P. Parusnikov. Project for the
Museum of the Revolution.*

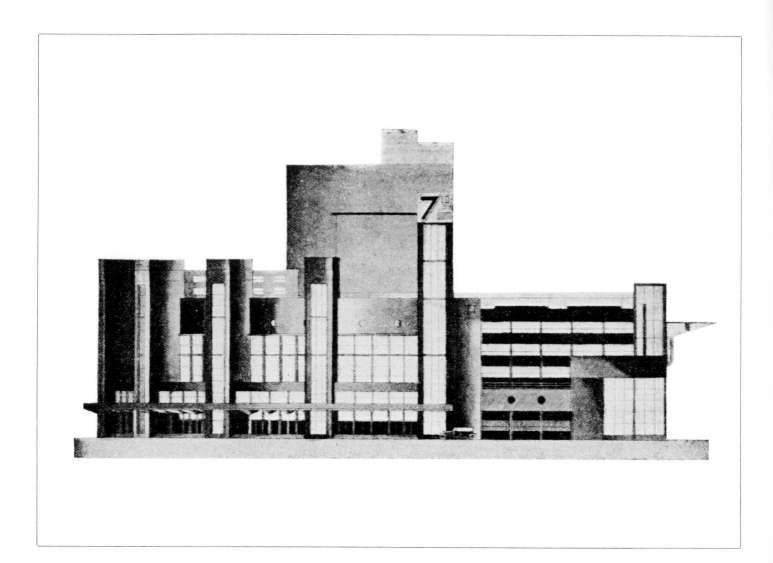

32 A. K. Burov. Project for a theater.

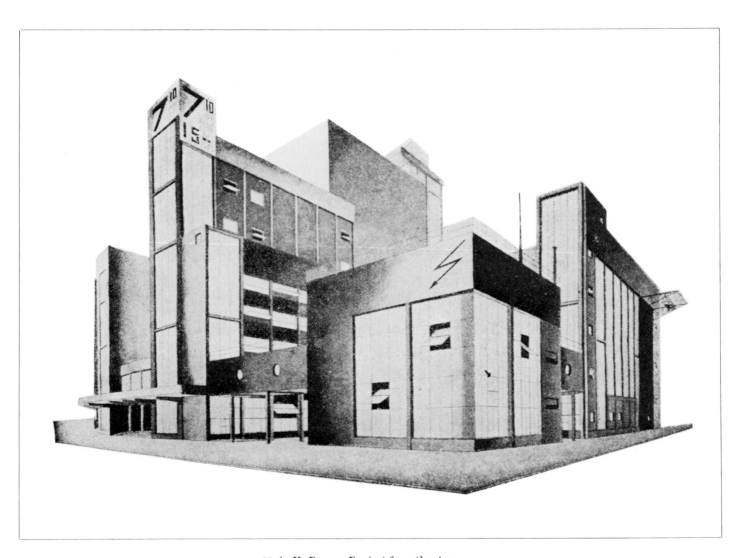

33 A. K. Burov. Project for a theater.

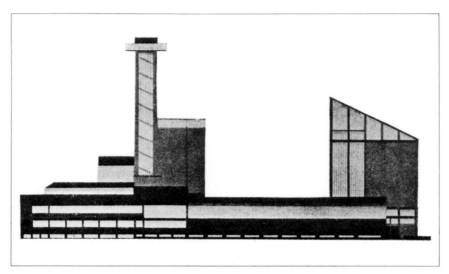

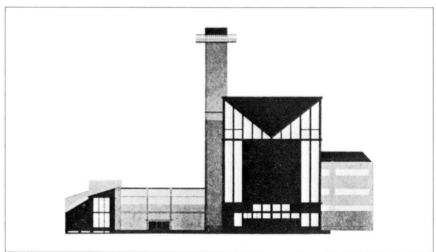

34 G. Vegman. Project for the Museum of Red Moscow.

35 G. Vegman. Project for the Museum of Red Moscow.

*36 G. Vegman. Project for the Museum of
Red Moscow.*

*38 V. Vladimirov. Project for a Universal
[Department] Store.*

*39 A. A. Exter and Gladkov. Izvestia
Pavilion at the Agricultural Exhibition
in Moscow.*

41 A. Gan. Vserokompom kiosk.

42 A. Gan. Vserokompom kiosk.

a. *Zavisimost'*. This word in Russian is usually taken to mean "dependence" or "reliance." However, as the context in which Ginzburg uses it throughout his discussion is more suggestive of phenomena being connected through an interrelationship of cause and effect, it is here and in what follows translated as "interdependence."

b. *Sobornost'*. "Collective social origins" is the closest English translation.

c. *Modern*. An abbreviated form of "Stile Moderne," this word is employed in Russian to mean the Art Nouveau.

d. *Dekadans*. The term "Decadence" was employed at the turn of the century in Russia, much like the term "Eclecticism" in Western Europe and the United States, to refer to styles composed of elements from various past historical periods; it was used pejoratively by those professing a modern approach to architecture.

e. *Samodovleemost'*. This word is usually taken to mean that quality residing in a phenomenon of being sufficient to satisfy its own needs, which is the sense in which the word is used here and throughout the work.

f. *Zhivopisnyi*. This word, like the German *malerisch*, can mean both "pictorial" and "picturesque." It is the former that Ginzburg has in mind, and given that he derives its usage from Wölfflin, it is here translated as "painterly," following M.D. Hottinger's English-language translation of Wölfflin's *Kunstgeschichtliche Grundbegriffe* (7th ed., 1932) as *Principles of Art History* (1932).

g. *Passeisty*. This word was used by Italian and Russian Futurists to describe those obsessed with the past.

Chapter Two

a. *Znachimost'*. Ginzburg uses this term a number of times to indicate an object's or phenomenon's act of, or potential for, signifying. The underlying concerns are analogous to those conveyed by Spengler's term "culture-symbol."

b. *Obshcheobiazatel'nyi*. This word means compulsory, binding, or compelling for all.

c. *Chastnost'*. The word literally means detail. However, Ginzburg uses it here in the particular sense of a small part that goes into making up a whole.

d. *Gipertrofirovannyi*. The word literally means "hypertrophied."

e. *Santil'bank*. This word, which does not exist in Russian, is one of numerous examples of Ginzburg's appropriations of foreign words, in this case from the Italian *saltimbanco* or French *saltimbanque*, meaning "acrobat" or "tumbler" as well as "mountebank."

f. *Piatno*. A word that means "spot," "patch," "blot," or "stain," with numerous nuances and applications. "Patch" comes closest to the particular sense in which Ginzburg uses the word, suggesting a surface area differing from its surroundings in nature or appearance.

g. *Italiiskoe*. It is likely that Ginzburg's misuse of the term "Italic" here and elsewhere in the text, including the chapter title, is not inadvertent but intentional. It seems to be calculated didactically to stress his contention, made in opposition to von Allesch's, that Italian aesthetic sensibilities were not forged from Hellenic ideals, but rather evolved out of the eclectic culture that developed in central Italy, a culture first encountered in Etruscan art and later augmented by the Romans. In a sense, of course, he has in mind the so-called Greco-Roman orbit of classical tradition.

h. *Degressivnyi*. No such word exists in Russian. The context suggests Ginzburg's adaptation of the foreign word "digressive," hence "aberrant."

i. *Klassitsizm*. This term is commonly used in Russian to denote the Neoclassical style, as in this instance, as well as classicism in general.

j. *Opornye kita*. A colloquial expression used to refer to persons of authority or high rank, a "big fish."

k. *Severo-Amerikanskie Soedinennye Shtaty*. Ginzburg clearly has in mind the United States of America (*Soedinennye Shtaty Ameriki*).

Chapter Three

a. *Kommunal'nyi dom*. This term has customarily been applied to communal housing, ranging historically from Fourier and Considérant's Phalanstery to the communal apartment houses (*doma-kommuny*) conceived in the initial fifteen years or so of Soviet rule. However, it can also mean "chapter house" or, generically, a cleric's dormitory, which is germane in the present context.

b. *Obshchestvo Britanskikh Arkhitektorov*. Ginzburg is obviously referring to the Royal (*Korolevskoe*) Society of British Architects.

c. *Arshin*. Russian measure, equivalent to twenty-eight inches or seventy-one centimeters.

Chapter Four

a. *Russkii stil'*. The so-called Russian style, also referred to more recently by scholars as the Neo-Russian style, emerged in the last quarter of the nineteenth century and encompassed numerous tendencies in the revival of indigenous aspects of Russian architecture dating chiefly from the sixteenth and seventeenth centuries. Significantly, the "freehand" aspect to which Ginzburg refers pejoratively was inherent in a good many of the original buildings and was not merely a contrivance of the style's practitioners, among the most notable of which was Aleksei V. Shchusev.

b. *Faktura.* As mentioned in the introduction (see p. 28), the word "facture," though scarcely used in English today, is the precise equivalent of the Russian. By facture, Ginzburg, like the Constructivists, has in mind a process of working a material from raw material to finished product in which its intrinsic properties are exploited.

c. *Fakturnyi.*

d. *Zhivopisnyi.* Again, the term "painterly" as well as the discussion of the underlying concept is drawn from Wölfflin.

e. *Modenatura.* Although this word does not exist in Russian, Ginzburg obviously is Russifying the French *modénature*, which denotes the profile of an architectural molding.

f. *Karre.* A transliteration of the French *carré*, not commonly used in Russian.

g. *Lokomobil'.* This now-rare word was used at the turn of the century to denote a self-propelling vehicle, one moving by its own power.

h. The three Vesnin brothers were Alexander A. (1883–1959), Victor A. (1882–1950), and Leonid A. (1880–1933). Their entry for the Palace of Soviets competition (1922–1923), though awarded third prize, was regarded by Ginzburg and others as the initial manifestation of an emerging "Constructivist" sensibility in Soviet architecture.

Chapter Five

a. "Rationalism" represented the other full-fledged avant-garde tendency in Soviet architecture in the 1920s. The Rationalist movement was established in 1920 and thus predated Constructivism by several years. It was founded by Nikolai A. Ladovsky (1881–1941) in collaboration with Nikolai V. Dokuchaev (1891–1944) and Vladimir F. Krinsky (1890–1971). It is striking that Ginzburg should be referring to both movements here with such evenhandedness. This attitude was to change considerably in the second half of the decade.

Chapter Seven

a. *Modenatura.*